SOUTH CENTRAL REGIONAL LIBRARY

Love Ya Like A Sister

A STORY OF FRIENDSHIP

From the Journals of Katie Ouriou

EDITED BY JULIE JOHNSTON

D0109717

Tundra Books

Correspondence © 1999, The Estate of Katie Ouriou
Additional Text © 1999, Julie Johnston

Published in Canada by Tundra Books,
McClelland & Stewart Young Readers,
481 University Avenue, Toronto, Ontario M5G 2E9

Published in the United States by
Tundra Books of Northern New York,
P.O. Box 1030, Plattsburgh, New York 12901

Library of Congress Catalog Number: 98-61728

All rights reserved. The use of any part of this publication
reproduced, transmitted in any form or by any means, electronic,
mechanical, photocopying, recording, or otherwise, or stored in a
retrieval system, without the prior written consent of the
publisher – or, in case of photocopying or other reprographic
copying, a licence from the Canadian Copyright Licensing Agency
– is an infringement of the copyright law.

Canadian Cataloguing in Publication Data

Ouriou, Katie, 1980-1996
  Love ya like a sister : a story of friendship

ISBN 0-88776-454-1

1. Ouriou, Katie, 1980-1996 – Correspondence. 2. Friendship –
Juvenile literature. I. Johnston, Julie, 1941- . II. Title.

BF724.3.F64O97 1999   j177'.62   C98-932832-5

We acknowledge the support of the Canada Council for the Arts
and the Ontario Arts Council for our publishing program.

We acknowledge the financial support of the Government of
Canada through the Book Publishing Industry Development
Program for our publishing activities.

Design by Ingrid Paulson

Printed and bound in Canada

1 2 3 4 5 6   04 03 02 01 00 99

In loving memory of our daughter and sister Katie

The publisher would like to thank the Ouriou family for permission to publish the correspondence and photographs of Katie Ouriou. Minor alterations have been made to the journals for consistency and clarity.

Looking Forward to Bad Times

★　★　★

CHRISTELLE OURIOU was thinking: "This place does not exist. I am not here. In one minute Katie will wake up and say, 'I just had this totally amazing dream!'"

Christelle, eighteen, was in a waiting room at the Hôpital Cochin, trying to focus on a book belonging to her sister, Katie. There were no windows, nothing to see; no people sounds, nothing to distract her. The intensive care unit – réanimation, as it was called over here – was in a separate building in a courtyard behind the main hospital. On the outside, the main building looked ancient, like everything else in Paris. Inside the annex, it was all modern – light, white, sterile. Insubstantial, she thought. Sci-fi. You would have no trouble losing track of time in here, although she knew it was still morning. Paris in the morning.

Overhead, fluorescent tubes glared, exposing sheer dread, peeling away Christelle's stability. She felt raw. Beside her was a stack of her sister's books. She picked up the quote book Katie had bought, with neat philosophic thoughts for every day of the year – her 'thought-du-jour' book. Katie's 'thing' was to memorize quotes, or copy them out and e-mail them to her friends. They were like little signposts pointing a way through life, and she *wanted to share them. Lots of times she'd try them out on Christelle, "Here's a good one for you. Want to hear it?" Christelle was usually deep in a book of her own, but would say, "Sure, whatever." And Katie would read out something like 'Friendship requires great communication between friends. Otherwise it can neither be born nor exist.'*

"Isn't that so true?" she'd say, and Christelle would usually agree. Katie was even amazing at making up her own 'quotes.' She had this knack for finding ideas that bounced like echoes off her life and everybody else's, too. Katie was a people-person.

Christelle was having trouble concentrating on the reality of the situation. Words were creeping around inside her mind: "My sister is unconscious. My sister is in a coma. My sister is – this was so hard to believe – brain-dead." Visions of Katie appeared, shifted, dissolved, reappeared – Katie doing her fitness run along narrow Parisian streets, laughing, sweating, her long hair knotted up out of the way; or en route to one of their suntanning spots, Champs de Mars near the Eiffel Tower, her beautiful red-brown hair loose, swinging out behind her as she walked; or Katie stretched out in the haze-filtered sunshine, propped up on her elbows, wrinkling her nose, muttering, "I hate my body." Remembering, Christelle clenched her hands, pressing down on her knuckles with her teeth. "Katie, you're not fat," she wanted to say, as she had so many times before, "you're not even chubby." In her mind she saw Katie leaning against a door frame, her arm draped carefully across her stomach, hiding any stray ounces of fat that might be lurking. She was a little taller than Christelle, and sure, she weighed a little more, but, actually, she had a great figure and a bustline Christelle envied. Pink cheeks, bright eyes; she bloomed.

"My sister's body is dying." The truth became as persistent as a headache pounding behind her eyes, forcing tears to the surface. Her mom and her dad were in the intensive care room with Katie, who had been put on life support systems. But it was a losing battle. Earlier, they had watched the doctor shake his head and say, "Only for a few hours she will be with you. Not very long."

Christelle was not yet ready to go in to see her sister, to face the reality of what was happening. It was funny the way she always thought of Katie as the older sister, even though she was two years younger. Whenever Christelle had a nightmare, she would climb into bed with Katie and, as long as even just her toe was touching Katie's leg, she knew she would be okay and could fall asleep.

Christelle turned pages, hoping to gain strength, or whatever it took, from Katie's books. What she was waiting for was a 'Katie-insight.' Katie believed people do things, or behave in a certain way, for a reason; that was the amateur-psychologist streak in her. She also believed things happen for a reason and if she searched hard enough through the words and beliefs of others, she would make sense of those reasons.

Christelle thumbed through the quote-of-the-day book and discovered that one of the pages was folded over. Not that this was anything new; Katie's books were almost all dog-eared. She was always finding things she loved and wanted to remember in practically every book she owned. She always marked the passages by flipping down the corners. Christelle read the quote for that date and looked up wide-eyed. "No way," she whispered. "This is too weird!"

Her parents came back into the waiting room looking years older than they were – red-eyed, exhausted. Her mother's forehead creased anxiously. "What's wrong?"

They were staring at her, shocked by the expression on her face.

She went over to them with the book. "This page is turned down!" She knew she was almost shouting. She let her voice drop and held out the book to her mother.

Susan Ouriou took it, nodding, saying yes, scanning the passage. "That's what Katie does. She's always turning down pages, isn't she? There isn't a single book that . . ."

"Maman! This is the only page! The only one turned down in the whole entire book!" Her mom was staring at her, not quite understanding. "Look at the date!" Susan straightened out the page and read the date, and then reread the passage.

That afternoon, after an illness of only a few days, unaware that her life was in any danger, Katie Ouriou died of a rare and swiftly moving leukemia, which had seemed, at first, no more virulent than the flu. The day was October 5, 1996 – the same as the date on the page that sometime recently, during the three months they'd been living in Paris, Katie had turned down. The passage for that date read: 'Going into the unknown is invariably frightening, but we learn what is significantly new only through adventures.'

Katie was sixteen.

*   *   *

The thrum inside Canadian Airlines flight 97 from London to Calgary magnified the hum inside Susan Ouriou's head. It seemed like days since they'd left Paris, although it had been only a few hours. Susan, Joël, and Christelle had flown from Paris to London and changed not just planes, but airlines. Everything seemed to take so long! She remembered how mired they'd been in rush hour traffic, following the hearse from the funeral parlor in Paris to the airport. She still felt trapped in that nightmare sluggishness, still felt she was moving through molasses.

Susan was exhausted. She asked the stewardess for water and found it to taste faintly of plastic. It struck her that grief has a sound and a taste and a texture. Her eyes felt gravelly, and the inside of her mouth was tender and metallic-tasting. She'd had too little sleep over the past six days. It had taken that long to wind up their affairs in Paris, to close up the furnished apartment they had been renting in the Rue Garibaldi, to arrange for Katie's body to be flown back to Canada. They had packed up the clothes they would need, or thought they would need, not knowing when or if they would return to Paris.

To spend the year in Paris had been a family dream, a chance to show Christelle and Katie something of their father's heritage, a chance to help them improve their French language skills. Susan and Jöel had investigated schools and the job market the previous summer and decided that it was a good year for them to go. As a computer systems analyst and consultant, Joël Ouriou could work almost as easily in Paris as in Calgary. Susan was an interpreter and translator and, after a few weeks of hunting, had found work in Paris. Christelle had just graduated from grade twelve and could easily wait a year before enrolling in a Canadian university. Katie had finished grade ten. She was to have attended a Parisian school for the equivalent of grade eleven, returning to Calgary for grade twelve to graduate with her friends.

The stewardess was asking Susan if she wanted a headset for the movie. She shook her head. Once the stewardess had moved on, Susan asked Joël to reach up into the overhead storage compartment for her carry-on bag. She pawed through it until she found what she wanted – a sheaf *of papers, e-mail messages, mostly. On impulse, Joël had printed them from the computer as they were packing to leave Paris. He had glanced at a few of them at the time and had called her into the room to have a look. At first they were both conscience-stricken about invading their daughter's privacy, but as they read on, they began to see a side of Katie they had never fully recognized. The messages, for the most part, were the outpourings of Katie's feelings and observations about friendship, her experiences in France – funny, sad, enriching, annoying – and about life, death, and spirituality. They were as personal as diary entries. In fact, this is exactly what they were meant to be. She had made a pact with her three best friends at home – Ashley, Maude, and Heather – that through their letters they would be each other's journal for the year of Katie's sojourn in France. There were over ninety pages of messages from Katie to her friends in Calgary, dating from her arrival in Paris on July 3rd right up to October 2nd, three days before she died. The last few messages were from Christelle to Katie's friends, telling them what was happening. And finally, there was a message from Ashley to Susan, Joël, and Christelle. If there was solace to be found in any of this, they had taken a measure of it from the experience Ashley described just after Katie's death.*

Susan riffled through the pages, through the earlier communiqués, reading random passages. They made her smile even though her eyes kept filling up. She began to read part of one addressed to Ashley:

In yesterday's e-mail, I told you how I'm totally into this spirituality thing. I've been reading all these quotes, and trying to apply them to my life. I made up one all by myself too. I'm quite proud. Here goes: There's a fine line between the risks we take to <u>live</u> life, and the ones we take to defy it. Tell me what you think, kay? I think you're really talented at that by the way, making sayings and quotes. It shows you have great insight. I'm feeling better by the way, not depressed I mean. I'm appreciating everything more. I realized yesterday that it's true, this year will go by fast. There's already only a BIT MORE THAN TEN MONTHS LEFT (sorry, every time I use caps lock I forget to take it off).

Susan paused in her reading to reflect on what Katie called her spirituality thing. Where had it come from? Neither she nor Joël was particularly religious; Joël had been raised a Catholic and she a Protestant, and the girls had been pretty well left to choose for themselves. Both girls had elected to go to St. Mary's, a Catholic high school, and both had become confirmed in the Catholic Church. Katie had been particularly struck by a book she'd found called Embraced by the Light, *by a woman who had had a near-death experience. She had loved this book, had wanted everyone she loved to read it – her family, her friends, her favorite teacher. Susan wondered, in reflective moments, if Katie hadn't been, in some unconscious way, preparing them all for . . . but who knows? How can anyone know? Katie had been searching for answers. That much Susan knew.*

She returned her attention to the page in her hand.

You should see how obsessed I am with music channels over here. I love them. (It's on right now, that's what made me think of it.) By the way, I think your goal for grade 11 is good, but don't start taking life too seriously, because you'll get bored. Focus on what's important to you, but leave time to go out a bit anyway, otherwise, you'll probably start to feel really isolated. It's possible to do it, just use me as your example (just kidding).

This country is OBSESSED with Macarena, it is ALWAYS on, it's a stupid bimbo version too. These are the things I have to deal with here. I'm proud of the culture over here though, with the fact that there actually is some. I love Canada, and it will always be home, but here there's a stronger heritage, and there's stuff here that's like unique to French people.

The last few paragraphs were about friendship. Friends had been Katie's world, although making friends and keeping them had not always come easily. She'd always been so super-sensitive about her relationships, imagining any slight as being out-and-out hostility.

Susan remembered Katie arriving home from school one day in tears; she must have been in grade six, or maybe, seven. "Everybody hates me," Katie had announced. "My friends all hate me." They had talked about this and it seemed to Susan that Katie had been trying to tell her friends everything she felt at a time when kids don't have much empathy for each other. She was getting laughed at. But she learned, got past it, started asking less of them and of herself. She began to live life more than question it, biding her time until her friends got to the point in their lives where they, too, needed feedback about their relationships.

Susan loosened her seat belt, flicked on the overhead light, and read a passage further down the page:

You know it's true we have this super special bond. I think that we were somehow meant to be friends, like our spirits have always been friends, and we chose to live our lives with each other (kind of) and to help each other. That's my opinion, hope you don't mind the cheese. I somehow can totally see that in our future we will always be friends. That's good, huh? It's like we're both so much on the same level of thinking, and we need each other to progress, or to understand who we're becoming. Yesterday, my sister and I were in this massive garden place, reading/suntanning, and I kept thinking about all this kind of stuff, and I was actually looking forward to times in our lives that would be harder, and where we would be there for each other and make our spirits stronger. I was looking forward to bad times!! That's strange, but it makes sense to me. I don't know about you.

ANYWAY, this message is pretty long and I just realized that your family could still read all this, and I feel kind of dumb, but hey, I'll deal with it. I love e-mail. Don't forget to save all the messages. Here's a few good quotes from my book for you, as my closing.

"If a friendship is vital, it's subject to change. In fact, it's vital only if it does change."

"Never fight with anyone you don't love."

"Friendship is to have the latchkey of another's mind."

And last but not least (for now anyway), in one of your letters you told me you wanted to be a beautiful person (you are by the way) and to have a perfect nature, and I want the exact same thing, but I think we should stick to this advice, "Don't try so much to form your character – it's like trying to pull open a tight, tender young rose. Live as you like best, and your character will take care of itself."

Love, KATIE

Susan let her head rest against the seat back. Something was taking shape in her mind, something she wanted to discuss with Joël, and with Christelle, who was sitting a few rows back. She felt such openness in these letters. She had had no concept of the extent to which Katie had been exploring ideas, making observations, expressing beliefs that often come only later in life. Her daughter had not been a saint by any stretch of the imagination, yet she had had a well-developed sense of right and wrong, justice and injustice. Susan let her eyes close, brooding, musing. Katie had been moral, but not judgmental. Susan remembered being disturbed by something Katie had done, or intended doing, and Katie had said, "If we only did the things you approve of, we'd turn out to be such wimps." And it's true, she thought. They have to test things, try things out for themselves to know what to keep and what to discard. "I'm a teenager," Katie had said. "It's my only opportunity to let loose."

As she read on, it occurred to Susan that the communiqués were more than just a recounting of day-to-day events. She saw that they contained a broader message about friendship, its bare bones, how it works. Could these letters be passed on to other people, she wondered, perhaps to other teenagers? What they seemed to be saying was, "You can be generous. You can share yourself and it's not going to diminish who you are." She wondered, briefly, what Katie's friends would think of this idea – Ashley, for instance, so pensive. She could see her now – tall and willowy, a slight stoop to her shoulders, smiling at her thoughts, pushing back a wisp of blond hair. And she pictured Maude – open, genuine, her petite, pretty Chinese features breaking into an infectious grin; and Heather – her brown hair as long as Katie's (twins, they had called themselves), quiet, putting other people's happiness before her own.

Besides sending e-mail messages from France, Katie had posted a ton of letters. Her friends would still have them. They might agree to share them. And there was Katie's journal. Susan dug into her carry-on again, found the journal, and opened it.

SUMMER 1996

Big updates to do, obviously. Let's just say that since my last entry, I've gone through grade 9 and grade 10, and am now beginning a year-long stay living in Paris.

Susan closed her eyes again and felt the nearest thing to peace she'd experienced since Katie's illness. It will be difficult, she thought, but not impossible. It can be done.

Best Buddies Forever

* * *

*H*OW TO *introduce Katie to strangers? Back in Calgary, moving through days like an automaton, Susan was sustained by the ritual of death and by its busyness. During the droning autumn weeks following the funeral, knowing they had to return to Paris at some point, she managed to hold herself together through total Katie-immersion, dwelling inside her daughter's journal and her correspondence with her friends. They were all willing to let her make what use of the letters she could.*

The more Susan worried about how to introduce Katie, the more she saw that Katie's own quirky personality leapt from the pages of her letters, especially from a year-old letter to Brad, a boy she liked, but scarcely knew at the time. Here was Katie, onstage, front and center, playing herself for Brad's benefit. Katie's passion had been acting. She'd had roles in a number of plays and had even, some while back, begun to consider acting as an eventual career possibility. "I want to be rich and famous," she had joked.

Susan was remembering something from the weeks before Katie died. The whole family had gone to see the movie Phenomenon, *and after it, Katie had said, "That's what I want to do." Susan had thought she meant be a rich and famous actress, but no. She explained herself very simply: "I'd like to make a difference in people's lives."*

Susan straightened out the letter to Brad. This is where she would start. Birthday cards and notes Katie had written months and weeks prior to leaving for Paris would come next. They helped set a stage of sorts, Susan thought, provide a backdrop. She began to type the collected correspondence, ignoring the October gale hurling rain at the windows, the air bitter with decaying leaves. It was like opening a door. She stepped over the threshold into the life of a young girl.

FROM A NOTE TO BRAD, FALL 1995:

You know, I did kind of have a bigger point in writing you this note. I know you already know this, but I think it would be somehow less awkward and grade sevenish if I told you myself. If you haven't already guessed, it's about how I like you. Like I said, I know you already knew that, but doesn't it seem better that now we don't have to be idiots and pretend that both of us are clueless and don't know anything? Plus it's so much easier to tell you in a note that it seemed like a good idea.

I know I don't really know you well or anything, and you don't know me, but because I wrote you, you have to write me back (just kidding). Seriously though, write me back please, and you can talk about yourself all you want, if you want to.

What can I tell you about me, let's see, I'm French because my dad is a pure Frenchman, and that's basically where all my family is too.

I was just looking around my room and I have this poster of these two angels that are drinking and smoking, and I love it, but that's weird cause it's not really me. What I mean is that I don't smoke, and I don't really drink (I had a bad experience that I'll tell you about sometime). I'm a warped teenager because the only thing I can stand the taste of (out of what I've had so far) is coolers.

Oh, I just remembered, Jen was showing me her pictures in Spanish (Spanish rocks, by the way), and she had one of you with a perm. I wasn't laughing or anything, but you looked so different. Give me one of your pictures for this year okay, and I'll give you one of mine if you want. I think last year's are better than this year's though, so you can have your pick.

Have you ever looked at *Where's Waldo* books? I was just wondering because that's what I'm writing your note on. Just so you know, sometimes things I say are just completely pointless and stupid (like the Waldo thing). Oh, this is wicked, my favorite song, "Dust on the Bottle," (yeah, it's country) is on. I'm taking a break to sing with it.

Okay, there you go, I'm done. This morning, I couldn't stand the kids I was babysitting for. Normally, I love kids, but they were just ticking me off because I was so tired (I started at 8:30 am!), and they were attacking me with pillows.

You know what, if you ever need to talk about your grandpa, don't feel stupid to talk to me. Andria's grandma died in grade eight (she lived with Andria's family), and it was really hard for her to deal with. I don't know why I'm telling you this, but it was actually really hard for all of us to deal with. In grade nine, on the anniversary of her gram's death, Andria completely broke down, and all of our little group of friends had to help her, although it was kinda hard to stay strong cause we were seriously scared she was suicidal. I could tell you this whole story in more detail, but I won't yet. Maybe someday if you're interested.

People in my family have died, but the hardest death for me to deal with was when one of the friends of our family killed herself. My mom is really sensitive, and it was really hard for her, which made it harder for me cause I try to be strong for her.

I'm sorry. I didn't mean to get into death or anything, but right now I seriously feel like I'm writing in a journal.

Okay, back to happy thoughts. One day, Brad, I'm gonna see one of your hockey games, okay? Hockey's actually a sport I can get into when I watch it. But of course, you have to come see my stage play too. I actually want people to laugh at me for some reason. No, I think I just want to believe that people are coming to see me because they think I'll be great.

This is a dumb question, but what's your last name? I honestly don't think I know.

Don't you love the outdoors, I mean it's cold and all, but nice huh? Now I'm just sitting in my backyard, listening to all my little neighbors frolic in their yards (I move around a lot, don't I?).

Okay, this is going to be my last page because, for your first note from me, you're already pretty privileged. If Ashley knew I was writing you this much, she'd be annoyed because she wrote me a note a while ago that I still haven't answered.

Oh, I went to the doctor's today, and my fingers are sprained from volleyball. You'll get to see their disgustingness on Monday, unless it's gone by then (right now, they're a purply green).

Did you know that I have a trampoline? I just thought I'd mention that interesting fact about me. People love my tramp. That's like the only thing to do at my house. We're the neighborhood entertainment too because we have tons of kids here, and they all wanna jump.

Okay, I'm ending this note now. I'm sorry it kinda dragged on, but what can I say, you're so easy to talk to. I hope you had a blast reading this. About the thing that was the main point of my letter, I hope we won't be all awkward now, and I didn't tell you to scare you or anything. Anyway, see ya later, write me back please.

P.S. – If you want to, call me sometime.

FROM A LETTER TO ASHLEY, OCTOBER 31, 1995:
Hey Ashley,

Well, happy B-day! Sorry my present was cheap and not longlasting, but I'm making up for it with this wicked note. This is longlasting. I was thinking you can keep it forever so you can reread it over and over (especially when I'm in France) so you can feel great, special, and happy.

Reasons why we're best friends (yes, it's cheesy but if it makes you laugh, go for it):

– We eat each other out of house and home (you have a slight lead over me in that area, just kidding)

– We can read each other like books (we're great psychoanalysts too)

– It's <u>never</u> awkward to talk to each other, unlike with others

– We talk about anything/everything and we always make each other laugh

– We never get in 'fights.' We can work everything out because we're awesome

– Whenever we're sick of others we only want to be with each other (except those few times when we're minutely sick of each other and that's okay)

– We're inseparable (ask anyone)

– I know all your secrets and you mine (even the gross, personal stuff, you know what I mean)

– Our families love each other and wonder what's up if we haven't talked to each other in the last five minutes

– We listen to each other, give great advice (like don't worry!) and you let me blab

How was that? Don't you just love me? Now, since you'll be reading this when I'm away too, I have to reassure you. We will <u>always</u> be great! At least in my mind. It'll be a long time to be gone, a whole year, but we'll both put in an effort to talk and communicate (Internet) with each other. In case you're in dire need of my helpful ears and brilliant advice, and I'm not readily available, here's this . . .

<u>Guys</u>

– You're beautiful. I'll show great pictures of you to French guys, and I'll write to you to say what their comments were (I won't lie either)

– You probably will have a guy soon, and if you're wanting another one, you shall have. Patience is the key, and you <u>must</u> talk

<u>Flirtation tips</u>

– As you know, I suck, no help to you here

<u>Family</u>

– It will pass, they really do love you. Everyone's moody sometimes, and my parents love you

<u>Drugs</u>

– Don't overdo it. Be careful, cautious, and if possible abstain

<u>Your 'I Don't Know Mood'</u>

– Get lost in your music, light candles, possibly incense, just relax and de-stress yourself. A bath is possible too

Fret not about me changing. I think I'm as me as I'm gonna get. I'll try not to worry about you either. If you ever have a really bad day, think of me in a full French school, with full French kids who'll think I'm a Canadian loser. I'll live though because it's just one year.

Do not forget that after high school, we have to go on a cruise and when we have our own apartments, we'll drink tea with each other. Don't worry, I will come to your hors-d'oeuvres parties so long as you're nice to my kids (yeah, I know you will be).

Anyway I leave you with the parting thought that you're my 'Beaches' buddy forever and always (like in the movie), and we'll never stop having our great talks.

À tout à l'heure

Luv ya lots, Katie BBF LYLAS

P.S. – I'll write more later if you want.

FROM A BIRTHDAY CARD TO MAUDE:
Don't let anyone read this, except A and H.
June 27, 1996
Dear Maude,

First of all, Happy Birthday! I picked the card for you because of the babies of course, aren't they so cute, just like our kids will be someday. Seeing that I'm going to be gone for a year, I have more to say to you than I normally would. Not that I don't always have tons to tell you, but that's beside the point. When I come back, you'll be driving (now that you're 16), and you'll probably have some wicked job, and who knows what else will change, but I honestly think despite any changes we go through, we'll still be able to be great friends, forever and always. (I know it sounds cheesy, but everything cheese-like that I write in here, I honestly mean.)

Maude, you know you are one of my few best friends, and I want you to know how much you truly mean to me. You honestly care about people. You're so open-minded, funny, beautiful, and intelligent, and I honestly think you're so wise. It's hard to explain what I mean by that, but basically you know what's really important about life even though sometimes you're too realistic, and you don't let yourself dream as much as you should.

You can do ANYTHING you want to, Maude. I believe in you, you should too. I don't know what I'm going to do without you for a whole year (if Ashley and Heather read this, the same applies to them). I know your life isn't easy, and things stress you out, with good reason, but try to remember that your family does love you as do your friends, especially me of course, and that even though I'll be in France, I'll still be there for you. Sometimes it's easier to write down what's wrong in your life, and I CARE MAUDE, so you can tell me all about it.

Look, I don't know if I'm gonna have a good time over there, mostly because I won't have you guys to comfort me, and to have great talks with, and to just have fun with. If you could come to France I wish you would so you could see me being a 'Parisienne.'

There's so many thoughts in my head for what to say to you, I LOVE YOU. YOU ARE A WICKED, INCREDIBLE person (oops, I forgot to capitalize). In memory of me next year, I say you should get involved in the drama dept. I know you want to, so go for it. Whenever you feel sad, read this card and write me. Here are other things to remember me by: the note on your mirror, listen to the song "I Believe" or Celine Dion (whichever reminds you more of me), look in your pantry for hours, complain about your life (my poor sister's going to be overloaded with my complaining since it'll be harder to moan to you about my life. Big loss, huh). If there's anything else you can think of that just screams KATIE!, do that too (oh yeah, you could go backpacking). Here's some last-minute advice to you: stay yourself, never change who you are for someone else, live each day to its full potential, REMEMBER KATIE, and most of all, you're 16 now, so just relax, take it easy, and have lots of fun. You've got your whole life ahead of you to, say, make babies and stuff (you have to wait for me though so our kids grow up together, Auntie Maude). I love you lots.

xoxo Katie O.

FROM JOURNAL ENTRY, SUMMER 1996:

Well, grade nine was fun with our little foursome in our loser class. We had a lot of fun/funny times (being in the play about Moses for one). And I won't ever forget our graduation from junior high or going out with my first boyfriend (Matt). That year, it felt like a lot was changing (first time I got 'drunk,' little vomit girl). I read *Embraced by the Light* that year and started doing a lot of thinking along spiritual lines. Ashley and I are now best friends (a process that started in grade 8), but my two other best friends are Maude and Heather. I love them, and if all goes as planned, we'll be friends forever.

Katie, Maude, Ashley, and friends at grade nine graduation

So, grade 10 now. The start of high school really wasn't that bad. Actually in retrospect, I loved grade 10. I will remember junior high as the awkward 'hell' years, where everyone's still very immature (especially guys), and there's a lot of backstabbing and general meanness going around. But, hey, I dealt with it, and here I am, better than before.

Grade 10 people are more mature (some), and I like how high school is structured better than junior high, where you don't just have one class all year.

I got my license near the end of the year and even drove Andria, Heather, and Lisa to my second rave, which was wicked I might add, although I was a bit stupid and smoked up at one point, where right after I had to drive. I learned though, and I'm not as stupid I hope.

Anyway, I loved the play I was in last fall. They were all beautiful people, and I had a blast, and I'll never forget all the nice things they said to me when it was over, and I hugged everyone goodbye, and I couldn't stop smiling, so they all thought I couldn't frown. Or the picture of us in our bras we took for Mark, or our warm-ups to "Get with the B-E-A-U-T-Y-Ooo, Ooo, Ooo, Ooo" (from that movie soundtrack).

Anyway, that's enough to get the ball rolling someday.

Besides that, in grade 10, I went out with three people: Brad, Andrew, and Kevin. I did a lot of embarrassing things during that time (train station kiss, going to the hockey game), but that's all in the past. Since then, Brad went out with Heather (which actually brought Heather and I closer), and I'm friends with him now. The past's forgotten, and we're good as friends. (Him and Heather broke up at the end of the year, but who knows, it might pick up again.) I went out with Andrew and we lasted a month surprisingly, but there wasn't much to it, and I started having mixed feelings and that's where Kevin comes in.

But I was leaving for Paris soon after, so we're both going our 'separate ways' while I'm here.

So, grade 10 also included making new friends, and being in school plays (Mrs. Darkways in *Weird is the Night*) and it was a lot of fun actually. I was put with people in grade 11 I didn't know, and I ended up integrating and becoming friends with the drama people.

Once this year, I ran out of gas on Macleod Trail, and this really nice man helped me out. He was wearing a Theatre Calgary shirt. That proves my point that drama people are great, nice, and funny (fun to be around). I hope I never stop acting in plays.

I should get some sleep now. I'll keep updating soon I hope.

Now I'm in Paris

★ ★ ★

FROM JOURNAL ENTRY, SUMMER 1996:

So, continuing right along. Now I'm in Paris. Quite a big change. Our parents decided that we should live out our French culture, at least for a year. Christelle's graduated now so she's trying for university here, whereas I don't really know what I want.

I want to be with people my own age, to hang out with, and to get to know Paris with, which would mean la première here, that's what grade eleven is called and it's pretty difficult. So next option is la seconde (grade ten), with people a year younger than me, which would still be really hard too. I'm not sure what to do, so I kind of want to put it up to God so that the right choice will come my way according to Him. I appreciate my friends back home so much. It's hard on me the way I miss them. I'm dealing with it, trying to go day by day, and appreciate as much as I can while we're here. We've already visited Le Musée de l'Homme and tons of other stuff. I actually feel I'm getting to know Paris. I can't wait to have friends though and do the stuff I really want to do, like raves, concerts, discos, bars, real Paris life let's say, with real Parisians. I mean, I know the Eiffel Tower by heart and all, but that's so touristic.

The real Parisian experience will come from doing all the cool stuff.

It's weird though. To think, right now, I'm in the André Citroën Park with Christelle, tanning and writing, and not in Calgary, thinking about going back to school in September.

My goals for this year are to get really fit, to improve my French and feel more French, to better myself as a person, like work on my selfishness and stuff like holding on to the past (grudges), and try to love and serve all people. And basically, to be more positive, and appreciate life, my good fortune, and this situation to the max.

I'll get good at typing, I hope, since I'm gonna start being an e-mail-aholic (with Ashley, Heather and Maude). I'll be such a good letter writer too. I told Ashley that she'd basically become my journal this year, and vice-versa. So, if my or her kids ever want to know something about this year, they'll probably have to read all the letters we wrote each other, unless I actually start being consistent with a journal (big doubts about that). It's too hot to write, adiós.

Sorting through the July correspondence, Susan found herself reliving the planning stage of their year abroad. They were able to leave their house in the hands of friends, who would live there for the year, and the Ourious themselves had been fortunate to find a furnished apartment to rent in a good district in Paris. The excitement and anticipation of adventure eventually outweighed Katie's concerns about being separated from her friends. There had been parties before they left and long farewells over the phone, and, at last, Susan, Joël, Christelle, and Katie had boarded a plane along with Susan's parents, who planned to tour in Switzerland.

After a night in their Paris apartment, they all packed themselves into a rented van and set off for Raindron – Joël's parents' farm and small vineyard near Angers in the Loire Valley – to attend a family wedding in early July. The wedding festivities over, they drove back to their apartment in Paris for a few days of sight-seeing before driving to Zurich, from whence Susan's parents embarked on their tour. Before returning to Paris, the Ourious visited friends in Annecy and Grenoble, heading back to Paris for a few days, and then driving to Switzerland again to visit with friends before picking up Susan's parents in Berne. After returning to Raindron for good-byes, they drove back to Paris and saw Susan's parents off on their flight back to Canada on July 28th. It had been a hectic month.

Susan, Katie's grandma, Joël, Christelle, and Katie taking a
break from shopping in Angers (near Raindron)

Katie's letters from France began in that early part of July 1996, on the drive to Raindron, before they had fully settled in to the apartment in Paris. Often the letters ran on for days, keeping each of her three friends, Ashley, Maude, and Heather, up-to-date, juggling information to avoid repeating it. In organizing the correspondence, Susan had to juggle the dates too, to keep each girl's series of letters in order. Katie continued writing all summer – long letters at the beginning, but eventually, once her friends became more familiar with the process, long e-mail messages. Katie began her first letter the day they arrived in Paris, before leaving for Raindron, continuing it after they got there.

LETTER TO ASHLEY, JULY 3, 1996:

Dear Ashley,

You should feel proud. I'm exhausted, yet writing you none the less. I am in my 'new' bed in our apartment at the moment, and I had to write you. This is my first night in Paris. I'm over the whole plane jet lag thing, etc. Guess what, Ash, I miss you. It's pretty well sinking in now, and I'm not sad yet, so much as disturbed. It doesn't feel right knowing that I can't just call you up all the time, and I know I can't clearly express everything in my writing. I'm already excited for you guys to come visit, but I dread starting school. You know how sometimes you get accustomed to feeling a certain way in a situation, and when it's all different-feeling, it's kinda scary, or sad. That's what this is. I'm used to a certain mind-set when going to France to visit my grandparents, say, and feeling a certain way here, and now I don't feel that way, and it's making me all screwed up.

Anyway, let me tell you about here. I have to admit it's pretty wicked. I didn't expect a lot of it. We have a big apartment (for what is normal) with high ceilings. We have a big screen TV with 9 channels (that's impressive). We have patio doors at the back that lead into a courtyard thing (think of school, but a bit smaller, and ivy growing up the walls). Across the way of the courtyard is another apartment (obviously), and they own a cat that I already befriended. Oh, we have a CD player too, and a bath (not just a shower), a microwave, dishwasher, a washing machine (but no dryer). Best of all, we're in a wicked district. I still haven't walked the streets, but I can see it rules. There are bakeries, cafés, restaurants and all kinds of stores everywhere. Plus parks, a fairly short walk to the really nice areas (Eiffel Tower, etc.), and a metro station like next door.

Okay, I'm sick of that. How are you? How was sailing lessons? (By the time you get this, they'll probably be over.) Are you seeing a lot of people lately, are you having fun? If not, you better try, just for me. By the way, the letter you gave me to read on the plane was superb (I'm so cool). I was laughing pretty hard at you, oh and with you. Let me just apologize because my letters won't be as humorous, c'est la vie, right!

Oh! I have an item of terrible news, we didn't bring a fax after all. I know, I know, it's horrible. Now you really have to e-mail me and send me your address (for e-mail).

Guess who I saw on the plane? No really, guess. Okay, I saw Madonna. Honest to God! Pregnant and all. This is no bull . . . well, yeah it is, but that's okay, our plane rides were so boring I had to make something up. Oh, by the way, my family hasn't read your letter yet, although I'm sure they will sometime soon.

Too tired to go on, write you later. (Goodnight, even though this will be completely irrelevant to you when you read it. I'm going to bed now in any case.)

                                                          smack

JULY 4, 1996

Well, right now I'm at Raindron (my grandparents' house). We just had lunch and now my sister and I are watching "Charlie's Angels," in French of course, and it's called "Drôle de dames." Pretty nifty, ain't it? Now that we're here it feels like we never left from last summer.

People in the seventies' shows wore ugly clothes, even Farrah Fawcett. She makes me sick, her smile is huge, and she has too many teeth! Okay, I'll get over it. Sorry, but I have to say this, Charlie's frigging angels are anorexic, they actually say they don't eat!

I know, I know, MOVING RIGHT ALONG (recognize that Ash? You only used it a thousand times). I'm only going to keep writing this letter till after my cousin's wedding, then I'll send it. I have to write to Heather, Maude, and Kevin too. Plus all my postcards, aiyaiyai! (Oh, but I am a dork.)

Why, may I ask, do French singers attempt to sing English songs?! They only have accents and say Baby over and over. I'm better today, by the way, less screwed up, maybe a bit more excited, but I'm feeling summery, so I'm forgetting the implications of a whole year. Although I do miss you guys.

At this moment, my sister is biting me. Tell Heather that made me think of her. Look, I'm boring you probably so buh-bye for now. Before I go, at the airport I bought a quote book, actually they're 'daily meditations.' I love them, I'll leave you with one (there's one for each day). Here's the one for July 11. "Greater awareness does not come in a single blinding flash of enlightenment. It comes slowly, piece by piece, and each piece must be worked for by the patient effort of study and observation of everything, including ourselves."

JULY 8, 1996

Sorry Ashley, I've been not writing you. Wait, what do you care? You can't really tell I didn't write you for a few days because you get to read it all at the same time. Sorry, just a stupid thought process.

Anyway, big stories for you. My cousin's wedding was really fun. I got drunk, danced a lot, talked to lots of people and was actually quite comfortable at it, etc. But then something happened. Didn't quite ruin my night, but did put quite a damper on my spirits for a good last portion of it. Remember that blonde guy Nicolas from my video pictures of last year, hair like Tin-tin? Anyway, he was there, but so was a friend of his. Actually he was a cousin on the bride's side.

In the beginning I was flattered because this guy thought I was attractive, but I still didn't really care. Then throughout the night, people kept reminding me of this, and he was extremely obvious, being quite flirtatious I guess. But we really didn't speak all that much to each other. We slow danced once, made small talk like, "Was leaving hard? So, you're living in France," that kind of stuff. Yet, get this. This dumb guy asked me out! We were walking outside – me, my sister, Nicolas, and him (Nicolas has had a steady girlfriend for like a year, by the way). He was asking me if my shoes were hurting (they were), then when we were not too far from the reception hall, in the parking lot in fact, he said (I'll give you the dialogue, sorry about my mix of French/English if there is any, just know it was actually all in French and not necessarily word for word.)

Him – "Je peux te parler avant que t'entres?"

Me – "D'accord."

Him – "Ça te dirait de sortir avec moi?"

Me – "Quoi!!"

Him – "Oui."

Me – "Je te connais pas, j'y vais vivre à Paris (and a lot of confused, stunned mumblings, like "Bah, euh, c'est que, etc.")

Him – "On aurait quand même une semaine avant que tu repartes pour Paris. Je vis pas loin de chez tes grandparents, blah, blah."

Me – (Shocked silence, kind of shaking my head)

Him – (Leans down and kisses me!!)

On top of that, he wouldn't let me pull away, it was so disgusting. Then I heard a car, so did he, and he stopped; I saw it was my parents coming back from somewhere, which it was, so I mumbled something like "I have to get my other shoes," and I went to the car. My parents left me the keys, and I sat in the car mumbling, "WHAT just happened," over and over again, not having a clue what to do.

Well, when I got out of the car, guess who was walking towards it. He walked right up to me and, while I was still completely unprepared with anything to say, he kissed me again. I should have bit his tongue off! Finally, I pushed him away and spoke to him with my head lowered so he wouldn't try to kiss me while I spoke. I was like pushed right up against the van, and I thought at that moment that this guy could hurt me.

Me – "Non, ça marche pas pour moi. Je peux pas."

Him – (In a condescending like he's speaking to a child voice) "Mais oui" (almost like it's only logical to be yes)

Me – "Non, je pars bientôt, j'avais un copain au Canada, et je peux pas faire ça si tôt."
Him – "Mais oui."
Me – "Mais non!"
Him – "Mais oui."
Me – "En disant 'mais oui' tu changes pas comment je sens, ça marche pas!" (Getting increasingly ticked off, dodging his mouth the whole time, honest to God, he couldn't take a hint)
Him – "Quoi?" (suddenly annoyed), "Tu m'aimes pas assez!"
Me – (exasperated) "Je ne te connais même pas!"
Him – "Mais oui on se connaît." (tries to kiss me)
Me – "Mais arrête!"

To shorten this, he kept saying "Mais oui" and trying to maul me. When I said we could never possibly see each other, he said we have tonite and tomorrow (my cousin's picnic). That ticked me right off because it was so obvious he only wanted one thing, so I got more angry and tried to walk away, but he said, in a pitiful little whiny voice . . . "Tu peux quand même me dire au revoir." Then he grabbed me and kissed me. For a full minute I was pushing at his chest. We were barely touching, except he held my head, but he didn't seem to understand that I didn't want him!!! I could add more stupid details, but after that I turned to walk back and he walked too, with his arm around my waist, and I was like, "Non, on sort pas ensemble." He was like, "T'es sûre?" I'm like, "Oui." We walked inside and practically ignored each other the rest of the night and the next day. At least I avoided him, he kept coming close.

So I had my first bad experience with a French guy. (That's what I told my mom, I told her the story, but not nearly as detailed or else she would've been scared.) He was one of those typical guys who are all like "C'mon baby, you owe it to me," or "Sure, it's okay." You can imagine how sick I felt. I honestly felt dirty.

Shocking story, huh? I couldn't believe it happened myself. Plus, when I went back inside, all the other young people somehow knew. They weren't bad about it really, they didn't care that much, but they were joking around with me like, "So did you have fun outside?" and I wanted to scream, "No!" but I didn't dare. I just smiled and shook my head, not really saying anything, although by the next day, most could tell by my ignoring him, etc., that I didn't have fun.

Okay, enough of that, I took up like almost 4 full pages with that story. There aren't really any more stories, for the time being, but I'll inform you when there are. Likewise, I hope. Just so you know, I'm not emotionally scarred or anything. I got over it, but when I remember, I get really mad again. I guess I never fully believed there could be guys like that, and now that I've been enlightened, I'm a bit turned off. It could take a few years to recover (yeah right, more like 2 weeks), I think that's about the time I'll be seeing Chris. (I don't think I told you, he's that guy whose cabin in British Columbia we went to, remember? The good-looking one from Western High. Well he's doing a French exchange with the two guys we met last year who sang that song on the video we made. Well, all three will be up in Canada right about now, but later they'll all come to France, and we're going to see them.) I'm proud, I remembered to close that with a parenthesis.

It's getting a bit chilly outside, I may have to go in soon (read Maude's letter to know where I am).

By the way Ash, I love you. I don't know if you're happy right now, but I hope you are. Now think happy thoughts, and do something productive because I know that will make you happy. Like climb the hill, or make a necklace, or make plans for tomorrow, whatever, just try to make the best out of however you're feeling. I don't have my quote book so I can't give you a quote, but I think "Don't worry, Be happy" applies pretty well to anything (recognize part of your own sound advice?). And if it so happens you're in a terrific mood, use this some other time to help, kay!

Well, I think I'm going to begin a letter to Kevin now (I actually do think about him quite a bit, too) before I go home to bed. (I'm still very tired lately, haven't had much sleep yet.) I'll finish tomorrow and send this away to you demain too (you should all get your letters at the same time).

JULY 9, 1996

Ash, I'm back in Paris now, and I'm so proud cause I had 2 letters waiting! (Brad, Lynley). I hope it's like this all year. Turns out it only takes about a week or less for mail to travel. This apartment we're in is so weird cause it's not like a house! Oh well, I'll deal with it. My parents are all stressed cause they want everything ready right away, but that's not possible with all we have to unpack, etc. I can't wait for you to come. We went for a walk in our neighborhood, and I want you to see me when I know how to buy things and know my friendly shop owners (except that they're not – friendly that is). I have to end now, I really want you to get this soon (you know the whole old-news thing). Know that I constantly think of you, I love you (so do <u>many</u> others), and I miss you. Think of me, but have fun, enjoy life, <u>don't</u> change. Love your best bud, Katie

P.S. – I think I'll put up that big picture of you on my wall. E-mail me from Maude's house too, alrighty! Keep smiling (please do Ash).

FROM A LETTER TO MAUDE, JULY 4, 1996:
Dear Maude,

I'm fine I guess, although feeling a little screwed up (read Ashley's letter to understand). Sorry I'm too lazy to really explain except to say that I know how much I'm going to miss you guys this whole year. This made me think, I don't ever want you guys to feel shafted if one of you gets a longer letter (Heather too), or learns different things. I suggest you all exchange letters so if I'm too lazy with one of you guys sometimes, I'll be assured that you still find out what's up. Tell Ashley and Heather this too.

Anyway, I feel immersed in French culture right now. I'm watching French 'rock' stars on TV. Pretty fun stuff I tell ya. There's a rapster called Doc Gyneco?! I don't know what's up with that, but he raps about his papa. . . . Okay, I'll stop. I'm a tad distracted now so I'll continue later, but first I leave you with this quote, "It is not impractical to consider seriously changing the rules of the game when the game is clearly killing you."

JULY 8, 1996

Well Maude, I'm listening to "I Believe" at the moment (I know you care), sitting on the grass by my grandparents' wine caves, surrounded by ducks (they're new) and chickens. I'm not feeling really good right now, about myself that is, and I'm missing you.

Anyway, I'm thinking I have to start to like my body someday soon or else I'm pretty screwed. No kidding, everyone here is skinny and wears tight clothes. There's naked, skinny women in every ad on TV, and I'm sick of it. I'll have to adjust and get used to myself to survive (no it's not that severe, I just feel kind of out of it).

Have you talked to Kevin? I do plan on writing him, but I don't think he'll tell me all. Sorry, I couldn't help myself.

I have to admit, I miss him more than I thought I would. Not nearly as much as you guys, but quite a bit all the same. This year I hope you'll keep me informed on gossip, even things including him. Please don't omit anything just because I went out with him.

Oh Maude! "Pour Que Tu M'aimes Encore" is coming on! I'm so happy, yet sad. I have no one to share it with. My sister doesn't really understand my passion for it.

Which reminds me, my sister told me I was really judgmental today. She insisted it was just an observation, a fact really, but I was insulted. I don't like to think I'm a snob who thinks she's so hot she belittles others, but it's probably true, so I'll deal with it.

You'd be surprised how often I think about how you told me you were jealous I was here for a year. Even with all my fears for the year itself, I'm actually more scared that when I get back, things'll be different, that we'll all have some kind of superficialness, and distance. Maybe we won't have anything to say to each other. Honestly, if I think about it enough, it scares me to death.

Guess what (lighter topic)? I had to sing at my cousin's wedding. My mom told people I was good, then they drew all this attention to me. I was like, "No!" (that was a bopper thing to write), so I went up and sang "Yesterday" (with the lyrics in front of me), but with 6 other people, so it wasn't really a big deal at all, I just felt like saying it. I'm doing a bit better at the social aspect up here, not amazing, but I'm progressing. You know what really sucks? I can never say all those witty, sarcastic things I normally would because I have no idea how. "Vole" is ON!!! Sorry, little interruption while I sing . . . Okay, sorry. Anyway, as I was saying, I don't know how to say "no offense," or any of those nifty expressions that help one express oneself. (I'm a loser, I'm well aware, don't worry.) I'm getting sick of little bugs crawling on this paper! (Don't worry, I made a point not to squish any on it.)

Well Maude, I want to send your letter away soon, and I know if I proceed to the next page I won't ever stop, so this is my last time writing you, in the very near future I mean. I have to finish Ashley's, Heather's, start Kevin's, and when we're back in Paris, I want to finish all my postcards (I'll send you one). I hope this letter wasn't too pointless for you, but that's me. I LOVE YOU, MISS YOU (even though the sinking-in thing is off and on), and hate not being able to speak to you. Write me back, pronto, have fun, be happy. Love Katie

(Answer all my questions, including Kevin issues.)

HAVE FUN ON YOUR CRUISE!!!

Write me!

JULY 17, 1996

Dear Ashley,

How's my 'Beaches' buddy? Every time I do anything, I want you there. I can't wait to show off Paris. Today I walked to Les Invalides with my sister (Napoleon's tomb), which is 10 minutes away. We are honestly in a good area. This morning me and my sister ran to the Eiffel Tower and back (aren't you proud of me) and made kind of a route. Now she wants to run every day, but I think I'll go every 2 days at the beginning. You just wait till you see me, by then I hope to be a skinny Parisian-looking girl, and I'll be very excited because you will surely have long, flowing blonde hair, right?

This whole writing thing is stressing me out. It costs a dollar a stamp for a 20g letter (up to that much weight) and more if it weighs more. It costs the same amount for a postcard, that's so absurd! Sometime I might buy postcards, write them, then send them all in an envelope to one person, who would have to deliver them for me. That person just might be you, you lucky girl. And of course, Curt wants me to get him a picture of Jim Morrison's grave . . . Aaah! My head hurts.

When it comes down to it, the only people I want to write is our little unit (you know what I mean). It would make my life a lot easier if Maude really figured out her e-mail so we wouldn't need letters. Actually Ash, you could figure out the whole e-mail thing too, that would be nice. If Heather did that too, my life would be considerably destressed, then I could write and receive from you guys almost every day. I'm "home" alone right now, the others went to our nearby supermarket, PrisUnic, for our din-din. Now, just to make you jealous, I'll let you know that I'm watching MTV (they have wicked cable). It's the European one though, c'est-à-dire, it's from London (it basically plays the same music though). All the DJs have English accents, and they play funny English commercials. You know what's ironic? France is publicizing Empire Records everywhere, the movie theaters are just now playing it.

We've been traveling recently (Switzerland, Grenoble, Annecy) in the mountains, it was so gorgeous. We're going back in 2 days to pick up my grandparents from their tour (Switzerland) and to stay overnight at our friends' place. Oh, I have another sunburn (very small though), and I'm getting darker. Considering this country is boiling, it makes sense.

Guess what, there's a new group called Backstreet Boys that are pretty big, honestly, they're a new New Kids on the Block right down to having a "hard core" guy, a cocky guy, and even have a babyface guy, who looks all innocent. OK, I know you care, it's just that their video's on.

I've been praying a lot lately. I'm determined to not lose that this year (my spirituality, that is). Plus, I've just wanted to pray. I really want to be happy this year. In this short time I've been gone, I've become more aware of how much my friends mean to me. I totally love you guys (you already know that I do).

Any boys with you in your sailing class, by the way? Hope so, and if not, the time will come (and you'll tell me all about it).

I just got home from exploring the Latin Quarter with my family (the fun place with musicians and tons of people around, especially young, good-looking people). Anyway, after our looong excursion tonite (it's 12:00 a.m. here now, we left after dinner), I'm beginning to question whether the male persuasion of Paris has any morals. No, really, it's actually annoying to have guys come on to you here. I didn't just bring this up, by the way, to sound conceited in saying that guys were coming on to me, but they were, although I was with my sister, and it was usually a double thing. My point is that they can be scary. Earlier on this month, guys came on to me and Christelle, and my parents (who were walking a fair distance behind us) freaked, my mom actually. Then I was annoyed because I found it flattering, and did our mom expect us to not go out so as to avoid it? Now, my perspective's changing. I know you're an eye contact person, Ash, as am I, and we both like doing that, but here you <u>don't</u> do that. I repeat, <u>do not</u> go there! Only because they start following you and saying stuff. I'm mighty sick of it already, but me and Christelle will just have to learn and become pros at shunning them. Probably thought you'd never hear me say that, huh? In any case, at the moment I'm actually too scared to go out at night without my parents (you have to try so much more for safety in this country), but <u>I know</u> the day will come when I do. Like when I have friends, guy friends especially, to go out with and protect me. Nice dream, isn't it?

You know when you're mostly asleep but awake, like you think you're having a conversation with someone, but you can't keep your eyes open so you try to mumble to them? I "dreamt" that I was phoning you, but it was really late here, and I was worried you were sailing. And I kept calling the operator because when she said, "Bonjour," I couldn't speak, I was so tired. I finally mumbled something but as the phone was ringing, I thought, "I'm wasting a call because I'm so tired I won't be able to speak to her." And so I "hung up" and went back to sleep. This all leads me to the fact that this phoning thing is bugging me. I want to call you (I know, already! you must be thinking), but I don't know when you're home, at what time to call (8 hours difference thing). I'll try eventually, but it won't be for another week or so anyway because of hectic travels (after Switzerland, we go back to Raindron, my grandparents' farm, for a few days, then Paris again).

Blah, Blah, Blah, that's all I do is blab to this paper. I want A PERSON! I hate this communication, it's so far away! Okay . . . my moment of bitterness has passed.

About goodbyes (I know that wasn't really our topic, but such is life). I'm sorry ours was so retarded, I honestly was so overwhelmed that night. Everyone was calling me, saying bye. I couldn't face it (nor did I want to), and I basically sucked. (Saying bye over the phone didn't help I suppose.) I hope you weren't mad or something. Maybe I'm making no sense right now, but I know you'll deal with it.

Hum, the thought of sleep is tempting me. I think I'll turn in right about now. Check ya later, skater (how gay).

JULY 18, 1996
Today is tragic because it was the day where that plane going from New York to Paris crashed. There was a group

of high school students in that plane. I hate this kind of thing. As you can see, I watched a fair amount of news today, mainly because I didn't go out at all, literally. Imagine, I'm in Paris, and I didn't leave the apartment once. I have my laziness to thank for that. The biggest thing I did today was e-mail Allison. Do you have any idea how much I miss being able to call my friends? Here, I basically am friendless, all I can do is write. I know I'm whining, I'll shut up now.

JULY 19, 1996

Well, right now it's lunchtime, and I'm yet again sitting in the backseat of our cramped rented van. And why am I writing you from the van you ask? Because, I tell you, we're going on another lame road trip, that's why. I have 6 hours of pure boredom, stiff legs, sore back, oh did I mention that my body parts are always falling asleep because I have to twist myself in dumb positions to fit in this rathole. Plus, my family "doesn't know" where my favorite tape is (the Celine Dion one I made at Maude's). I told them if I can't find it, I'm going back to Canada. Did you know that if ever we do have to go back (financial reasons), we'll have to live at my Calgary grandparents' house! Wouldn't that be a long year? Our house is being used by some friends of ours. I sincerely doubt that will happen though, so I'll live. Okay, the car ride's bumpy, I'll write when I have more patience.

JULY 21, 1996

Well, today we left Switzerland (I'm in the van now, surprisingly enough), and I will tell you about our stay there. We stayed at our friends' big apartment, who have 2 kids, one a guy my age, but a basically friendly geek, and a girl about 2 years younger. The girl wasn't there, but the guy,

Gaspard, had an exchange guy from Wales staying there. (Pretty good-looking, with an English accent!) So our first night Gaspard wasn't there, so we kind of got acquainted with Andrew (that was his name). The next day we went to the beach, all 4 of us (parents came later), and later that night all of us went to their friends' party by a lake (that's where they lived). Anyway, Gaspard was playing games most of the time, so my sister and I were usually alone with Andrew (he actually has wicked big blue eyes). You'll be happy to know I talked about you a lot. Here's why – he plays the drums and is in two bands, so I told him your drum story, how you took 2 lessons and quit. He lives in the countryside, in a small village, on a farm. I kept saying, "My friend Ashley lives in the country . . ." and would make comparisons with his country life. Plus, I told a lot

Katie, Gaspard, Andrew, and Christelle in Switzerland

of stories about our friends, so although I don't remember, I know you were in them a lot. He wants to become a vet, with farm-type animals (he has assisted with a cow cesarean). He rides horses, he has a wicked voice, deep and English, big blue eyes. He loves dogs, I think. Although I'm not sure you care, he could teach you drums, etc. Even as I was planning telling you all about him last night, I thought, how pointless, because we'll never see him again. But we exchanged addresses, so we could go to Wales someday, or he to Paris, or Canada (I said Canada would be better). Who knows though, we'll have to see.

Enough of that. At the party yesterday, it was really weird. You see, Switzerland has 2 big languages, French and Swiss-German. Our friends are French, but at the party the majority of people were Swiss-German. Therefore, I understood nothing. Quite a few people spoke French, but some not very well, and the only other people our ages preferred not to speak French (German being their mother tongue and all). So Christelle, Andrew, Gaspard (he kind of understood), and I were clueless. It's neat, though, how people have different languages. We sometimes understood their meaning by their gestures, . . . but never exactly what they were saying, unless it was French. There was this guy there, honest to God, I stared almost all night. He was our age, maybe a bit younger, and he was so hot, he was honestly sexy. You know when you see one of those guys who just automatically make you go, "Wow!", well that was it. He was so perfect, but his name almost made me laugh when I found out what it was, it was Fabio. Honestly, he doesn't look <u>anything</u> like that, by the way. Don't get any brutal images.

Aaaaaaaaaah!!! This is our worst trip ever. If I thought other days were brutal, this just takes the cake. (Yes, Katie is a dork.) First we woke up at 6:00 (went to bed at 2:00), drove for about 2 hours to get my grandparents, and are now proceeding to go, not just to Paris, but to the farm (chez Mémère and Pépère). I only have 6 hours, possibly more, left, really. I'm quite happy. Oh, and it just so happens that this trip, I'm feeling carsick. Oh yes, I could throw up out this window, but I won't. Of course I never felt sick when it was a 2 hour drive and when there was room in the van to vary our seating plan (the very back, which is where I'm stuck, makes me feel the worst). Did I tell you that at the beach I got sunburned, not a thorough sunburn, just streaks here and there over the front and back of my legs.

I wonder what you're thinking as you read this. Is it excruciatingly boring? Oh well, if it were, you'd deal with it.

Oh, I forgot to tell you that I also told Andrew (hee, hee) how our friends are obsessed with English accents (myself included), and how you imitate one A LOT, and your mommy says you sound like Princess Di, Princess of WALES I might remind you. I know you're probably embarrassed, but don't worry, he's never met you, he didn't care, he was quite amused actually.

Hello Ashley, just wanted to let you know that your accent's excellent and to keep it up. Like Katie I'm bored out of my mind and my bum's asleep. Just thought I'd let you know. Christelle

What a cool cat that one is. Okay, cool cat wants the pen for her letter, so I'm stopping for a bit.

(Later). Nighttime at my grandparents' farm, there's my setting for you. I'm tired but too lazy to go up to bed. I realized something, despite my burn I am also tanned. Amazing, but my arms are tanned, my face too. I love it, it makes my arm hair less noticeable. This sucks because I <u>know</u> this summer I'll get the most tan I ever have, and you'll miss it. Maybe I'll send a picture.

43

I'm feeling very discouraged. I looked at the e-mail with my dad, and I still have no messages. That's all I ask, I tell you. What if something really horrible happened, like someone died (better not be you), and I know nothing. Unless you guys get off your butts with that e-mail, I swear I'm gonna die. Maybe everyone's on vacation, yeah that sounds good, it'll make me feel better for a few days anyway. Okay so, Ciao (people say that to me) for tonight anyway. I need sleep. Oh, but first, my Beaches pal, I hope you remember to journalize your life for me too because, you see, I care, and I want to stay updated. Painfully enough for you, that's what I'm doing. You have to do it too. Taa-taa!

JULY 24, 1996

I have to end this letter soon, it's a tad long and will probably be expensive. Anyway, we just got back to Paris, and I came home to a letter from you and from Kevin. Anyway, your story was very interesting about that woman on "Dini Petty" who got in touch with her past lives, like when she knew she had once been Gwenever. I suggest you buy the book though and let me read it, maybe bring it when you visit, how's that, because I have sincere doubts that I'll be able to get it here. The book I read about past lives in was by Jude Devereaux. I think it was called *Eternity* (or *Destiny*), but I know the lovers' names are Talis and Calissandra. Just look around and try and find it. I think a good idea from now on would be that whenever we write letters, we say exactly what day we got the other person's letter, so eventually we will know exactly how long it takes, etc.

You know how sometimes you collect thoughts in your head, to remember what you want to tell your friends, or have conversations with people about? Well, all those things I collect and think about are all directed to my sister now, instead of being able to disperse them among my friends, over the phone or whatnot, so she's quite sick of me. Not to mention that she doesn't respond to my liking, so sometimes I get frustrated too, but, as my mommy says, such is life!

She just came into my room (my mom) and informed me that we're going out tonite to eat. That's fine and dandy, except I look awful. Oh well.

Like this paper? This is my last page so appreciate the beauty.

In Kevin's letter, when he mentioned his posse of friends (the ones not from our school), I cringed, but already I don't really remember what it felt like to be going out with him (I'm not sure that makes sense, I mean there's a distance between us, it's totally not the same). Kay, well, I'll sign off now,

Love Katie BFF LYLAS XOXO

P.S. – Tell Maude I keep sending her e-mail. (My family misses you too.)

JULY 26, 1996
Dear Ash,

Here I go again. I just can't stop writing you (my grand-parents left today). I got your letter today, and I was happy to learn all about your sailing and stuff. When I'm more adjusted, I'm gonna start using my computer for writing letters. What's really strange is that the majority of the things you told me about, what you think about, your goals, etc., are the exact same things I've been thinking about, honestly. Recently I've been reading this French book called *Bernadette Soubirous*, which is about a girl who saw the Virgin Mary, and because of it, I've been thinking about that whole sex after marriage thing. I really want to keep writing, but it'll have to wait cause my sister and I are going to Jim Morrison's grave today, on the metro, all by ourselves. I bet you're proud. I don't even care, but I promised Curt I'd go for him, so I will.

Later on – Well, I accomplished my mission, but the picture might suck, it was hard to get. After doing that though, my sister and I explored other parts of the cemetery. It's a really weird one, all the tombs are packed together, some huge, some small. I think you have to be rich for a plot there. Some families have small house/chapel-type things, where their whole family's buried, and a lot of it is very old, 1800 and earlier, so it's weird to think that these families, or people buried there, are like people we read about in our romance novels. You can't help but wonder about what these people were like, their history. It's actually an interesting cemetery. I'll take you there. I've already started a list, "Things to do and see in Paris," so I'll refer to it when you guys come. I can't wait, that image you had of us sitting in a café, all stylish, it's gonna happen, baby.

Anyway, tonite my family went over to our new neighbors' house (one of them) and had a drink. It was really good because they're so nice and they have a twenty-year-old daughter who's so nice, and I think we'll even go out with her since you can go anywhere, despite age. She seems willing and I can't wait. I'll finally learn how to be a Parisian.

Well before, I was telling you how much we're totally in sync, it's true. And all those guys harassing you, well it's like here, it's honestly the same thing. Weird, huh?

Anyway, I liked the prediction you gave me for 96/97. I'll read it all several times I'm sure, but here's the part I like best. "Flashes of insight and understanding will help you make hard decisions. Your life will be quiet until all of a sudden, exciting events will occur that require overnight decisions. Expect the unexpected and listen to your inner self."

Did I tell you that at the airport I bought a book called *The Book of Life*? It's totally yours and my kind of thing. There's all kinds of "meditations" which tell about and analyze things like love, passion, creativity, ideas. I think it will teach me a lot this year, and I'll be an even better psychologist type when I get back. I'll have to show it to you. Enough for now, I'll write later.

JULY 27, 1996

Well dearie, I'm so proud of you. My family read your letter today (the one you gave me to read on the plane) and after, my mom said you should be a writer, that you're extremely creative (and funny), and that she wishes she could write like you, and she was being honest. I'm also proud because you've set some good goals for yourself, and I believe you can do it if you really want to. Like be a pro skier, or sailor, and then you can teach me, and then we can ski in the Swiss Alps, or sail in the Mediterranean Sea. And I'll find some family friends to lodge us, unless we're rich. I can't wait for all the things I want to do, life honestly seems too short to pack it all in.

Anyway, today my family went to the massive library here, and honestly, I'll go back because I want to expand my knowledge, my insight, my culture, my awareness. Every day my motto will be Carpe Diem (seize the day), and I'll take advantage of the Paris life and Europe. Maybe (probably) with school they'll offer a trip to London or something, and I'll go. My family definitely will take every possible opportunity to travel somewhere neat, like Greece or India. Real travelers inspire me, people who take in a broad spectrum of life and develop open minds about people, religions, etc.

Oh, I'd also like to tell you that I'm really proud of your honor roll status, and I know you can keep it up. You know my cool little book about life? Well, I started reading it, and because of it I can see you are a very insightful person. I always thought it but, although I'm not there yet, there's topics I'd like to discuss, like whether thoughts and feelings are linked. . . . Before I go to bed, I'll leave you with some of the subject titles for certain days: Subtle Truth, Words Create Limitations, Observation Without Thought, Freedom From Fear, In Death Is Immortality. It's really interesting and so us, don't ya think? (We could have great discussions on this stuff.)

JULY 30, 1996

Well, first, I must tell you that I'm lying in the Champs de Mars (in front of the Eiffel Tower) writing to you. Honest to God. What a charmed life she must lead, is what you must be thinking. But that's not quite right. I may be doing this now, but the first half of the day was spent bawling in my room. That's right, today was the first time I cried because I want to go home. I'm okay now I guess, it was really a bunch of things accumulated that made me break down. Mostly, missing all you guys and my life at home, but also stress for school, stress for the exam I have to take that will decide which school, what grade I'll be in, etc. (I take the test after school starts by the way), and stress for the correspondence courses I'm taking to prepare for the stupid test. (I'm taking French and math, and it's hard! Their math is like grade eleven math for us, and I'm supposed to learn it all in a month!) Plus, all the usual things I get upset about. I'm sure you can figure it out.

What I really don't like here is the immense lack of privacy. Every member of my family came and had a talk with me while I was incoherent, whereas I hate that. If I wanna talk, I will, but my bawling has always been personal, with my door locked, and the music full blast. It just feels so different, it's frustrating, besides I've always had my fits and got better on my own, or with assistance from you guys, but now, when I'm on the verge, I can't call you up to take my mind off it. This will all just take some adjustment, I'll survive.

I hope your e-mail's coming along, I reeeaaally want to use it. Christelle and her friend Heather communicate every day, and I want that. It could become routine.

Oh-oh, clouds are forming, it might pour on us. Oh well, c'est la vie. You know, my parents love you so much. Especially after my mom read your letter, she wanted me to tell you that you made her laugh and cry (almost all your sentimental stuff to me really touched her). After (I already told you, I know), she said you're really talented, etc., and she felt guilty for taking me away from such great friends (she said it plurally, but it stemmed from talking about you). If ever your parents are on your case, just think, Katie's parents love me.

But I forgot to tell you about the rest of my day. After my session, my family said we should go out, so we went to our "mairie" (look it up if you care) and got all kinds of info and things on our district (programs, courses, sports clubs, theaters, etc.), so I'll be busy here, especially considering I'll go to school 5 days a week (possibly Sat. morning too) from 8:00-5:00 or 6:00. ISN'T THAT BRUTAL!!! But hey, there's also the guaranteed 2 hours of homework every night I've been told about. No problem, knowing me this shouldn't plague, disturb, or depress me at all. No way, José (Ha, Ha, Ha, what witty sarcasm).

Enough of that, who cares? What I wanted to mention was that one advantage to all that school time, as we found out at the mairie, is the amount of vacation all these French people get. School starts Sept. 11 (me later, thanx to my stupid exam), then in Nov., they get about 2 weeks, X-mas is from Dec. 21 to Jan. 6, then in Feb. they get about 2 weeks, and spring break is from April 5 to 21 (mark that down and let me know when your spring break is as soon as possible because we have to start to organize soon). Plus they get another week or 2 somewhere, but I don't remember where. School ends June 28. Just so you know, that's basically my year. Don't be offended, but my friend Katie might come in Nov. for holidays. I know she wants to come and her mom doesn't mind her missing school. So you guys might not be the first, but when you come, I'll have had more practice, and we'll all have missed each other more.

AAAH!!!

You'll never guess what just happened. It's so ugly and gross!!! Oh my God, I have bird shit all in my hair and on my shirt!! Honest! It's so scary!! It's all over and I'm all icky. I must clean now. My sister sucks, she can't help me. She's laughing too much, and she's spastic.

(I'm writing now. It's Christelle. Katie's on the ground. She must get out of her tee-shirt – it's all over her back. It's BIG and green and the white stuff is in her hair. She's such a dirty, dirty girl. Why us, she says? She's calling me unhelpful – of course I'm helping – I'm writing.)

Okay, I'm back. I'm traumatized, I'm icky, and I need a shower, but I am sitting in the Champs de Mars. I can't even change decently so I put a shirt over to cover the disgusting mess (luckily I can't see it, or I'd cry). Can't you just imagine being me? The spaz you would have taken would have scared me, especially if you were wearing your Victoria's Secret tank top.

Ironically, before this fiasco, I was going to tell you something that happened just 2 minutes before. A gross 30-year-old man came up to us and said, "Que vous êtes belles, couchées là." Of course, I was the one facing him so I just looked, then turned back to my paper. Then the jerk said, "Est-ce que je pourrais rester là avec vous?" Icckk! So I go, "Non," and he's like, "Oh, d'accord," with this attitude problem, and he walks off muttering who knows what. Maybe, "I'll stalk you and kill you in your sleep then." Then a bird shitted on me, this day is oh so lovely. I'm going home now because we're late, and I'm icky.

It's later on now, and I just survived an embarrassing moment. My parents made me and my sister go to our neighbors' house alone and invite her to dinner for tomorrow. How awkward! It wasn't that bad. We came in, invited her, then she invited us to come in for a drink. We did, then after a little bit, her incredibly good-looking boyfriend came downstairs and sat with us. It was very obvious that we'd interrupted something. I swear I was red practically the whole time. Plus, once I used a wrong expression and must have sounded like an idiot. I am improving though. So yeah, we left, feeling like fools and wanting to kill our parents, but hey, we survived <u>and</u> we accomplished our mission. Gotta burn the warts on my feet now so I'll get back to you.

JULY 31, 1996

I'm sending this today, so I'll end now (you and Maude are both getting one). So know this as I send you away, I love you and miss you incredibly, as you already know. So enjoy your summer, W/B when you can, pray for me and all of us, and I hope you and Maude have more time to spend with each other soon, cause she really misses you.

Love you forever and ever, Katie

JULY 30, 1996
(You always have cool paper)
Dear Maude,

I just received the letter you wrote on your funky paper, thank you very much. Ironically enough, just yesterday I was totally depressed and complaining about feeling like everyone forgot about me already. Letters take so long, that's why even though I've already told you, I really want you to start e-mailing me so we can become regulars and do it every day. Okay, that's the only time I'll say it in this letter, but Pleeaase do.

First I hope you're not still upset about not seeing much of Ashley and Heather because of your job. Whatever you do, have faith. Everything will fall back into place when things settle down for all of you. Meanwhile, don't fret and enjoy what you're doing at the Y. Trust me, you will achieve your goals of having kids love you all summer. You're super with kids, always have been, and I think you'll be a wicked mother someday. (Just be patient, Maude, I don't want to come back to you being pregnant or anything. JK.)

I know what you mean about liking having kids love you though. It actually upsets me when kids I babysit don't. I actually feel hurt. But I loved, for example, when one girl I babysat hated when I left, and she always told me she loved me and that she wanted to be my little sister.

It seems weird to be so unconnected to all you guys and your lives. I mean like day to day, realizing what's going on and stuff. It's kind of depressing, but that's cause I miss you all so much. Things are so different here for me. I'm aware that this could be good for me, but at the same time, it's sad. My sister and I get along really well, but we both have always had separate friends and lives from each other, but here we're alone. August looks like it will be <u>really</u> long, and I'll probably cry every two days, but I'll keep hoping and exploring (I do get out, don't worry), and it would be good if I Expect the Unexpected, like Ashley says, because maybe that means I'll unexpectedly meet some cool young Parisians to hang out with, and hopefully take my mind off my worries for school.

I think I might be PMSing right now because stuff is really getting to me, but also because this is a BIG adjustment, and it offers many difficult situations I've never dealt with before.

Otherwise, Paris is moving along fine despite my problems. I know how to walk to the Eiffel Tower by heart I've

Katie in front of the Eiffel Tower

done it so much, and every day I learn something new about this massive city that is now my home. It's exciting, but not nearly as fun as it would be with more friends. We're constantly seeing my <u>parents</u>' friends or relatives that, unlike you, I've now seen often enough to be a bit (quite) bored of their company.

JULY 31, 1996

Guess what, Baby! I just received the other letter (from your plane trip)! I'm so happy! I read it already, and let me tell you, I understand your being sick of planes. On our flight this year I didn't even have fun, none of the plane excitement I mean. Something tells me that on the flight home though, I'll be pretty excited, of course. You know how I make up dreams? Well I've imagined my homecoming so many times now. It's weird cause I don't want to make up any dreams about this year yet. Because I honestly still don't know what I'm going to be facing, and just in case, I don't want to get my hopes up. So instead, I imagine when I'm back in Calgary.

If I were you, I'd be scared of American Airlines and anything from the States after the TWA accident. That was really sad, the United States have no safety left anymore.

I'm watching MTV right now (from London). I assure you, I won't lose my English this year. I've never fully explained this to anyone yet, so you can be the lucky one. Concerning school, I now want to go into their 11th grade (la première) rather than 10th (la seconde). But my problem is that I first have to pass a test so they can see where I fit. If I get la première, I'd take a première littéraire which means that languages are basically their focus. Math and science you do less of (that's really good, trust me). Plus for languages, I'd have a lot of French (obviously), an English

class, and another English class, which would be appro-
fondi (more difficult). If I go to the school I want to go to,
that English class would probably consist of other for-
eigners. Apparently another Canadian, a New Yorker, and
stuff are going to that school. That could be fun, and hopefully still easy. What's good too is that I'd probably get to
travel with my English classes to England or the States (I'd
pick England). But the problem is I can't know anything
until after that dumb test, which is at least a week after
school starts, so that might suck. But, maybe I might be
lucky because my mom went to the Ambassade today to
get an attestation for my sister that says she has an equivalent to the Baccalaureate (their diploma). So she's going to
get one for me for la seconde so I could go to la première,
without writing a test maybe. Pray for me, kay, cause that
would be the best thing to happen.

I still really don't think I'm going to change this year,
except maybe with superficial things (looks, accent). But I
can't know anything till school starts, cause that's where
influences lie, although I know who I am, and I don't plan
on changing unless for the better. Same better go for you
though, okay.

I hope everything goes well with your grandma. I know
it's hard to deal with, but I think you should tell her you
love her, maybe even in Chinese, so you won't ever feel
guilty about that, although I'm sure she knows it. Unfortunately, death is a part of life, and we're going to have to
deal with it many times during our lives, so I think we have
to learn to not fear it, despite the fact that we know it will
cause us much pain when loved ones die. Okay, depressing
topic. Oh, the news is on, and it's making me sad too. They
just showed a big funeral, a memorial they held (in Paris)
for victims of the TWA. Actually it was held for 5 people

from the same family who died, the youngest 15 years old, and all his friends from school came. That must be so hard to deal with.

Okay, so that's really enough now. Hey, guess what? I'm trying to be good at exercising here. My sister and I have a run to the Eiffel Tower and back (she also has a harder one I can't do yet), and I want to get really good. You know what I really like here, the Notre Dame Cathedral. One Sunday (not during summer though, too touristy) my family's going to go to a mass there. It would be so beautiful, and I like praying there. (I've decided to go today.) I went once and prayed for all our friends and for me to have a good year. It would mean a lot to me if you would pray for me for that reason. Maybe somehow it would make this year easier. I love you lots, for forever and ever, and I think of you every day (at least).

Love Katie

P.S. – Please tell Heather I e-mailed her, she has to check it and write back.

AUGUST 5, 1996
Dear Ash,

I just spent the last 20 minutes crying, listening to the tape I made at Maude's house. I was crying (kinda still am) cause I got your most recent letter today and I can't believe how much I miss you. I miss everything. Everything here scares me, it's all so uncertain and yet, everything back home scares me too. I'm scared that you don't need me anymore, that everyone forgot about me, and that maybe when I get back home, I won't belong anymore. Don't tell her, because I'm also glad you're not lonely, but I'm totally afraid that Heather is taking my place. I don't feel anything against her cause I miss her too. I'm just saying, I'm scared that things won't be the same anymore. I'm sorry to be telling you all this, but I told you you were going to be like my journal. It's been a few days since I talked to you guys on the phone now. Was it just me, or was it a bit weird for us? I'm sure if we had had the means to talk longer, we would have been normal, but there was so much pressure to say all we wanted to say. In any case, it was good to hear your voices again.

I regret somewhat now not having realized what was going to happen before I left. Everything makes me bawl now, honestly it's like every second day. By the end of the year I'm going to be beyond spiritual, God hears from me so much. Truly though, I feel my belief getting stronger. All kinds of things happen to strengthen my belief, but I'm too lazy to try and describe them.

Okay, let's just face it, I'm feeling miserable. We all imagined my life here being at least remotely exciting, but it's really not, not yet anyway. I actually feel bad because I don't ever really have anything exciting to say. Meanwhile, you always have something to tell me, and I always feel like I should be there. It's a most frustrating feeling. The most eventful thing I have to tell you is that the day you called me, well that night, my sister and I went to our neighbor's house (the girl Mathilde) because she invited us to a gathering with her friends. So we went, and we were surrounded by 12 20-year-old guys and Mathilde. At first it was awkward, but then I started talking to some guys (my French is a lot better by the way, and I think, from what people tell me, I'm already losing my "Canadian" accent). Anyway, everyone there was smoking up, but I didn't. I fear that here people don't make it a point to get drunk. It's almost pointless because it's not illegal to drink anything, they can do it anywhere. On the other hand, they're always smoking up (that's my guess) and smoking. I really don't want to get into all that that much while I'm here, so it kind of bugs me.

(Later, nighttime)

As the heading said, it's later. I spent the day entertaining kids. Remember my mom's friend Genevieve who has 2 kids, Katie and Nicholas, and Katie is the one who really liked the hot tub jets in Jasper? Well, anyway, they're spending the night here. Today, we all walked to the Champs de Mars (you should be quite familiar with that place now) to the kids' playgrounds there. Now I have an adorable story, and you must also tell Maude because I know how she loves kids. On the rope dome thing, these 2 little girls were talking with their cute accents and skill (which greatly exceeds my own). The cute little black girl was like, "On va chanter la chanson de . . . de . . . tu sais, ah, oui, Céline Dion." I was already listening, but then my ears perked up even more. The cute white girl was like, "Ok, I'll start and then you come in." But she didn't know all the words, so the little black girl sang most of it herself, which was "Pour que tu m'aimes encore." It was so cute, I felt like it could have been me and one of you guys doing that together and, ironically, it was the song that had made me cry the hardest this morning, although the girls' rendition cheered me up. One of those heavenly signs I keep getting that I somehow think means something.

On the other hand, today little Katie was lifting my shirt and, when she saw my tummy, she said, "It's all fat," even though she adores me and thinks I'm pretty (she said that, I'm not just going for conceit). Anyway, it was pretty unsettling because, without a doubt, I know that kids are fundamentally honest. It's true, kids tell it like it is and always have. So basically, I still have to lose weight, but hey, Rome wasn't built in a day.

I'm feeling a bit better by the way, although I realize it can hit me again, full force, without warning. Expect the unexpected, right? It's weird though cause sometimes I totally appreciate what we're doing here, like when I actually feel like we're living a Parisian-type life (there is no typical Parisian life). When I walk down a street exploring and think it's beautiful, when I learn something new about the city, or just anything interesting (did you know if you took 30 seconds looking at every piece of art in the Louvre, you'd have to be there for 3 months). Things like that, that make me proud of here. I was disappointed

Susan, Katie, Christelle, and Joël by the Louvre

thinking that I won't get to show you guys around Paris much, to show off my knowledge and stuff, under the new circumstances. Why can't two countries have their vacations at the same time?!

AUGUST 7, 1996
(nighttime)

How sad. I think my trusty pen is dying on me, then again maybe not. Who cares, right? First, tonight my family went to the Latin Quarter again, but my sister and I went to see a movie, *Safe Passage*, with Susan Sarandon (seen it?). It's really good, so real life somehow. I love Susan Sarandon, she's the wickedest actress, she's my idol. There's hot guys in it too. I strongly advise you to see it (it was subtitled, by the way). Moving right along, did you know our Celine Dion is calling it quits next year? No more singing. You probably do, you are in Canada after all, but I just think it's a tragedy. Maybe she wants a baby.

Today I finished my roll of film (finally!) from end of school and stuff. Tomorrow we'll go develop it (takes a couple of days though), and I took pictures of my room. If they work, I'll send them to you, just to give you some idea of where I am, if ever you try to imagine. But all that must wait.

Besides that, I spent the rest of the day watching TV and writing a "Commentaire composé sur la littérature." Pure unadulterated excitement (hint of sarcasm). Oh well, I'm now done my second French homework assignment, just 2 more left (next one's a dissertation). Oh yeah, and 3 more math homeworks, but that's just scary. I got my marks back for the first one, not <u>too</u> bad for French people, but get this, 8/20 isn't <u>too</u> bad for them.

I was listening to my little tapes yesterday, and me and my sister were laughing at you (no offense). You'll

60

understand when you hear it someday. I love you, don't worry (like you will).

AUGUST 11, 1996

Today we had a phone call, remember? Anyway, this was my day: talk to you, go back to bed, wake up, go running, come back home, do abs, weights, and stuff in front of MTV (I love that channel. I actually know more about the global music scene now than Andria, she'd be choked). Then, had lunch, showered, spent a torturous hour doing math, then my mom got a brilliant idea to walk to these gardens around here. So, although I was in a bad mood (math), we went and I brought my CD player so I could be left alone with my music. That's what happened till it started to pour. In less than 5 minutes, I was literally soaked, as if I'd jumped in a pool with my clothes on. All my clothes became tight, some see-thru, and I was most uncomfortable. Oh well, now I'm dry, except my hair, and just sitting at home.

I just realized, when we're in grade 12, the drama department will be so dead. That's a sad thing I think, but maybe I'll be active if I have any time between settling back in, doing all catch-up work, trying to get a job, maybe auditioning for Storybook again, and mostly having a social life. Did I tell you how I'm not sure I want to really be a psychologist anymore? Obviously not, I haven't told anyone. I still want to get a psychology degree, just in case, but I kind of want to have my own day care, but it'd be special cause I'd be allowed to counsel people's kids if I felt they needed it. I don't really know though, as always, there's so much I want to do, I don't know how to do it all.

I'll hopefully send this tomorrow. I want you to get it before you go on holiday.

AUGUST 12, 1996

Well, last night I was surprised to get a call from Maude. I'm so happy, I got 2 calls in one day! I love talking to you guys, I wish it didn't cost anything though. So now, I'm sending the negatives of my pictures to you too, cause there's some from the end of school too if you want them (you or Maude or Heather), but screen them, cause I look gross in all of them so don't show them to many people.

Katie, Ashley, and Heather "studying" after school

Oh yeah, I forgot to tell both you and Maude this, but I might also see the Cranberries here, and maybe . . . Celine Dion. Yup, again, but most of her songs would be in French this time. It'd be interesting to see what changes, and also may be disturbing, cause I liked her so much the first time. Ooh, "Ironic" is on MTV.

Soon I have to do my math, and later this aft I might

run as it's rainy and probably we won't do anything very significant.

Holy depressing, I'm watching a French music channel, and they're doing a "love" segment. There's all these cute couples, although there's also cute couples all over Paris, sitting on park benches and making out. Typical, don't you think? It's the city of love after all.

I probably won't write for a little while, cause I know you'll be gone, and I'm actually going to the farm again soon, then to the sea for a whole day (yippee). Anyway, I hope this reaches you soon, and thanks again for calling me. As always I love and miss you. Actually, last night I was so happy for having 2 calls and stuff, and I was thinking about what wicked people my friends are and – sorry for the cheese – but I thanked God for that. Then I asked God to bless you guys, and I will do the same all year, and pray that you guys have a great year. I do have to do my math now, so adieu. Hope you like the pictures (the ones of my room are kind of demented-looking, the walls look so white and big for some reason), and if you want you can develop the negatives. Keep in mind I look gross though, kay.

Love, Katie BFF LYLAS

P.S. – Hi from my family. My best wishes to everyone. Tell Heather I'm sending her letter after I get hers.

Finally Logged On

* * *

THOSE NEXT frustrating weeks! Susan was recalling August and September as she continued to collect and organize Katie's correspondence. At the time, she had been busy in Paris, seeking employment as an interpreter, and both she and Joël were kept in never-ending turmoil trying to sort out schooling for their daughters. To fill her time and as a way of meeting young people, Christelle decided to take a university history course. Getting her enrolled at the Sorbonne, and getting Katie prepared for the equivalent of grade eleven in a Parisian public school became almost a full-time occupation.

Back in Calgary Katie's friends had been engaged in their summer activities – Ashley and Heather took sailing lessons together; then Ashley went with her family to a summer cottage on the Shuswap, and Heather worked in a dance supplies shop. Maude went first on a Caribbean cruise with her family, and then worked as a counselor at a Y day camp. Katie continued to write copiously through the summer, but now her thoughts were poured out into the family computer and dispersed via e-mail.

64

SUBJECT: Hey Ash
SENT: 15/8/96 9:36 AM

I got both your test messages this morning. So you're finally logged on. I'm not going to write much cause I want to be sure that you receive my messages first, then we can start to really e-mail, kay. So write back as soon as you can, so I know you know how.

Katie

P.S. – It's Christelle's b-day today, she's 18! **Hello Ashley, it's the 18 year old. Glad you've finally figured out your computer! Bye.**

SUBJECT: I got it all Ash
SENT: 16/8/96 9:41 AM

It's working Ash!! I'm so happy. Well it's Friday the 16th here, and I just woke up and did my daily routine of checking e-mail, and for regular mail. I might run today, but maybe not because my cousins are here, and we'll probably do a lot of walking anyway. We're going to Notre Dame, again, but that's okay cause iat's so nice. Did I ever tell you that one time when my sister, this girl Jennifer, and I went there, some man tried to convert us into Mormons? It's a strange little story, but maybe for another time.

So, is your family enjoying this e-mail too? I'll try not to say anything embarrassing if they are. But I feel like telling you that last night, my sister was quite unhappy (18 b-day really sucked here), so we talked till late about life kind of. Then I was so into it I wanted to read *Embraced by the Light* again, so I started. I still love it! It's neat too cause things make more sense this time, and some things have more meaning. There's so much more I want to say, but I feel awkward, so I'll keep it in mind until you've written back and told me if I have a reason to feel awkward, you know. Anyway, have a lovely day (you're sleeping right now). I'll write soon, kay.

I miss you tons (you know that),

Love, Katie

SUBJECT: Hello Ashley
SENT: 17/8/96 9:00 AM

HI ASHLEY!!!

Guess what I just found out? You know that guy Chris whose cabin we went to in British Columbia? Well, he has been in France this last month on an exchange thing with those French guys I told you about. Anyway I just found out that all of them, including parents, might be staying here for a night or two. We'll see, but I'll keep you updated if that happens. I'm sure it would be quite an adventure. Wow, I'm typing fast. So remember from now on to check more closely for e-mails from me.

Today, I plan on doing math (of course) and then my family's going to a museum. That can be very interesting. The other day, my dad, sister, and I went to the Museum of Man. It was cool. There were all these neat exhibits on just humans, and then on all different cultures and heritages of man. You might want to visit that when you come, and of course, you can conveniently walk to it from our house. Maybe I could take you guys to school someday.

You know what I still have to do when I get home? Read *The Celestine Prophecy*. I hope the Jude Devereaux book is the one I told you about. It's gonna make you cry if it is. Oh, I'll give you a small outline of things you said on the tape, that me and my sister were laughing at. "I'm home alone . . ., I'm eating a muffin now . . ., I talked to (so and so) on the phone today . . ., I just found out Mike thinks he has me wrapped around his little finger, etc.," but most of it was funny because of the way you said it, pretty much a monotone, and it was also the pure pointlessness of it. That's okay though, it's fun for me.

SUBJECT: Hello my dear twin
SENT: 17/8/96 4:59 PM
TO: Heather

Hello my sweetie,

I obviously got your recent e-mail, and I was quite happy. Ashley tells me you guys will have a relaxed year, wearing fleece, and not caring about makeup. You should see, I already wear almost no makeup here. It's really not worth it. In Canada, it seems more like a faux pas if you don't, but not here. By the time you guys come, you'll fit right in. Anyway, I miss you tons, and I hope we keep up this e-mailing, cause it's cheaper and much quicker than normal mail. If you know how, by the way, try to save all the e-mails. Next year we could print them, like notes. Until I get an answer (which better be pronto), have fun, even in Calgary (JK), and know that I truly miss you.

LOVE KATIE

SUBJECT: Heather in Calgary
SENT: 19/8/96 10:38 AM

Well, your subject heading is much better than mine, but I guess Paris made all the difference. Your letter hasn't got here yet, that's not your fault. It's the post people, it'll get here though. I pity you guys cause school starts soon.

Mine starts Sept. 11, except my test I have to take to get into school is Sept. 19, or something like that. Somehow though, my parents are going to try to put me in school for the days in between, even though I won't be signed up. Good for you, by the way, for being over Brad. I think it's great that you guys are still friends though.

Today I'm going tanning with Christelle, and we're starting our video of Paris. Trying to keep busy you see. Pretty soon though, my family is going to my grandparents' farm again, but you can keep e-mailing cause we bring our laptop baby everywhere. I am being consistent with my running, as I'm sure you are with exercising at Lindsay Park. Just wait till you can drive there, it'll be so much easier, guaranteed.

I think it's really good that you guys kept yourselves busy with sailing for so long. It's always sad when something fun like that ends, I know. Don't worry though, soon you'll be kept busy with school soap operas, and all the new grade 10's (ha, ha, jk). No, really, make the best out of this year, and have fun while we're still young and don't have any big responsibilities, or stresses, because they'll be coming someday (let's not think about that, shall we). It does seem weird that you guys will be going back to school, to regular routine, pretty soon, and I won't be there. I can't help but wonder if anything will feel different. I guess you guys will have to tell me. Anyway, I have to jet (we have a strict timetable for today, cause we don't want to miss our favorite TV show). I'm going to be such a wicked typer by the end of this year, that's good, huh? So, bye bye, remember to try and save this if you can, and write back if you get it. Love you lots, and miss you lots too.

LOVE KATIE

SUBJECT: You rock Maude
SENT: 20/8/96 11:19 AM

HI MAUDIE,

I'm so happy right now. I just got your e-mails and, on top of that, I got a letter from you today, and one yesterday too. I plan on writing back letter-style soon too, but honestly, time here is starting to feel limited. That's to say, every day, we never have enough time to do all that we want and have to do. Oh well, like Krista said in her letter (I got it yesterday too), it's best to stay busy.

Let me tell you, Maude, that I think you are the sweetest girl. In all your letters and e-mails you are so sweet, and you say such nice things, that I could cry. I won't though cause I wouldn't want you to think I'm sad. I'm actually doing a lot better you know. At the beginning it's hardest, I think. Being able to communicate with you guys so much, and in so many different ways, makes me happy. Don't worry, by the way, you always think you haven't written enough, but at the moment, I've gotten the most letters from you. I'm always thrilled, but I don't want you to feel like it's some big obligation, or that I'll be mad if you can't for a while. Anyway, soon we'll be all competent with the e-mail, so if you don't want to write letters, you don't have to. Unless, for personal reasons, you feel it's safer to write in a letter, although I assure you, my family doesn't read my e-mail unless I let them. You'll have to tell me how careful I'll have to be though, where your family's concerned.

First of all, I'm worried about you. What is this problem you're having? Whatever it is, I'm sure it's nothing we can't handle. Tell me in e-mail if you want, because your mom might not let you call, and I'm scared of calling cause I don't know when you're home. Oh, by the way, yesterday I got the sparkly letter. You are so talented, sweetie. No really, that was so sweet of you, and I put it up in my room. You're right you know, our relationship won't change this year I'm gone, I'm sure of it now, and it's weird, but I already have only a bit more than ten months left. With that realization, I really want to make the best of this experience. I've been to some museums, and learning all this stuff about France and Paris, and hopefully becoming more cultured. I want to broaden my horizons when I'm here, have fun, and learn. That's what life's all about, isn't it?

I think you have some kind of mission with kids, my dear. Whether it's just that you'll be a terrific mother (which I'm sure you will), or if you're going to help them in other ways too, I don't know, but you'll be great. Don't stress about what you're going to do. I think when school starts you should ask the counselors about different jobs, or careers that are kid-oriented, to get you thinking. Persevere, baby, and you'll find what you want. I agree with you, too, that kids have this way of making me feel bad if they don't like me, or if they're mad at me, that they tell things like they see them, see truth more clearly than we do, so if they don't like me, I feel like they know something more than I do. That deep down I must be bad, because the kid can see it. That's a bit weird, but maybe you understand what I mean.

Actually, the hardest thing for me to deal with here is the unknown, mostly not knowing anything about school and friends here upsets me. When I'm stressed it's because I'm thinking about math or school subjects that deep down I know don't really have to matter. I don't want you to worry about me because I'll be fine. Nor do I want you to miss me too much, even though it touched me in your letter all the nice things you told me. Know that we will have long lives, and hopefully we will be more together than apart. Sometimes you may want me to come back (as I do sometimes), but at least this way we're learning to deal with something that's difficult and will help us later in our lives. We can make it, baby, I know it. I want to console you with other matters you put in your letters, but I may just write you because it might be too personal to risk on e-mail.

I know this doesn't mean much, but I totally understand how you'll feel when your work ends. I've told you this before, but it just amazes me how much your work sounds like my stage play. I was never unhappy in drama, and it was like a family, almost like an escape, with people you really get along with. And it's sad when it ends. On the last day of *Babes in Toyland*, so many people were crying, and it was so touching, I will always have great memories from that, but I will hopefully do more plays, where it'll happen again. You will probably work in that kind of situation again too, now that you've known it.

Well, I have to go now. We're going out with Chris and the two French guys, and I have to shower and stuff. Unfortunately, I won't have time for writing letters today, but I hope this e-mail gets sent to you OK, and that you know how to read it. I love you so much, always will, and although I miss you, at the same time when I think of my best friends, I get very happy. Your memories are very comforting. I hope to hear from you soon, but I'll understand if time is thin (like me), so don't worry about insulting me and stuff. God bless you too, Maude, (I keep praying for you guys lately, I'm big on praying now). Be happy and enjoy yourself. Live life to the fullest, day by day, and you'll be okay.

LOVE KATIE, XOXOXO

AUGUST 20, 1996

Dear Maude,

Today was a really good day. In the morning I got your e-mail (I'm so proud of you!), and my family spent the day with fun people. I love people, they make the world go round (dumb thing to say I know, but I'm happy). Anyway, we went up the Eiffel Tower with 10 other people. First of all my dad's friend Didier, his two sons and wife, then Didier's friend Jacques, his two sons and wife, and then this guy (you know the hot one, Chris) and girl from Calgary. The girl's name was Kylie. And the two exchange guys, Mathieu (I don't know how he spells it) and Laurent. We talked a lot to Kylie, and surprisingly to Chris, too. (He used to be mute. It seemed this time that he actually wanted to make conversation with me.) I felt bad because

Katie, Kylie, Chris, and Christelle in the Latin Quarter

we neglected Mathieu and Laurent a bit, but the Canadians leave tomorrow, so Mathieu and Laurent, I think, are going to spend two days with us. I won't feel bad then, plus they're really nice, and funny. All this to say that I had a good time, and I felt really self-confident. I spoke to everyone and I felt so sure of myself, I loved it, so I hope you're proud of me. (Later we went to Père Lachaise again, then to the Latin Quarter at night.)

Okay, sorry, that might seem like wasted space, but I just had to jot down my happiness. I think Chris is so attractive, and he was being really nice to me. Let's just say it boosted the old self-esteem.

I wanted to write you a nice letter too because I want you to know how much I love you. I sincerely do. Like, it almost feels like unconditional love. I want you to know that throughout the course of your life, I want you to be able to depend on me when you need it, and sometimes you will, and that doesn't make you weak. I want you to learn not to feel vulnerable with me, cause you know I will always be there for you, over oceans and kilometers too. I wouldn't ever want to hurt you. You are a beautiful person, inside and out, although you don't see it that way, I sincerely do, and you can do anything with your life. Go day by day, finding happiness, a bright side to each one, and you'll never have a bleak future (I know it can be tough advice to follow, I'm still trying).

I feel bad cause you're worrying about you and Matt breaking up someday, and what it will do to your friendship. I thought about the dilemma, actually put myself in your position, and I could totally understand. All I could think of, though, is that the best relationships come from friendships, like you guys, and I think "if" a difficult situation ever came up, your friendship could always conquer. Sounds dumb, but when something's important to you,

you instinctively fight for it. You're capable of that, Maude, but don't worry about it now. Just enjoy yourself and appreciate what you have, while you have it. That's my advice, for now, whether you want it or not! (jk)

Seriously, your letters make me feel so special. Letters like yours, and Ashley's too, definitely help me out. I really do trust that you guys will still be there when I get back, and everything looks better after that. I'll keep writing later, sweetie, my sister "needs" me to turn out my light (time for bed, you understand). Ta-ta.

AUGUST 21, 1996

Guess what I forgot to tell you yesterday? At the restaurant we went to I tried escargot. In all honesty, it didn't taste that bad, but the texture was all weird, and I had to eat it fast and not look at it while I still had the courage. I don't think I'll eat it again though. I still think it's gross, I mean, it's a snail! My mom would kill me if she knew I was writing you and not doing my French or my math homework. Too bad for her. I just spent the last half hour or so reading about how to write a dissertation. Now I'm supposed to write one, but I just don't care. I didn't come here to bore myself out of my mind, now did I? Which reminds me that my family's going to my grandparents' farm soon, yeah, what fun! (jk) I don't really mind though, I can tan and since I won't really have anything better to do, I'll do homework I'm sure. Just so you know, I'm still basically happy right now. I started writing Ashley a new letter today too, and I am overflowing with love for my babies (you)! I don't know what's come over me, but I love knowing that my friends are great people. My family thinks so too. For a while my mom felt guilty for taking me away from such great people (her words).

AUGUST 22, 1996

Ma chère Maude,

You want to know what's so cool? In the apartments across from us (they are across our "backyard," you'll understand what I mean someday), our neighbors in like the third apartment are always playing classical and jazz music, and it's so beautiful, it fills the "yard," and we open our windows to hear better. But what's really cool is that it's not being played by a CD, someone's actually playing the piano. And they're honestly mega talented, like a concert pianist. Someday I'll tape it on my little tapes so you'll see what I mean. Just think, it could be someone famous, and the music is so beautiful. Sorry, I'm all moved because he/she is playing as I write, and it's amazing. I feel like I'm at the Jubilee or something, getting lost in beautiful music. Actually it's kind of like how you felt about the opera in your e-mail. I WISH YOU COULD HEAR THIS!!!

We've got it so good at the apartment, I can't believe it sometimes. Our only problems here have to do with the "living," like school, work, etc. But everything else is good. I figure it's meant to be, and God is making sure everything will work out great in the long run. I'm being really close to God lately. I just kind of spring that on you, but I'm rereading *Embraced by the Light* and praying a lot, and I just love Him. I really want my life to be balanced, physically, mentally, emotionally, and spiritually. I'm working on spiritually right now, as you can tell, and I think it's good for me. Spiritually doesn't necessarily have to mean that you're sure of your faith in God, but more that you acknowledge the fact that you have a spirit, and without spirit, we are nothing, and God helps nourish our spirit. There's a little analyzing for you, dear. Sometimes it just comes over me you know.

I now know it's a man that plays the piano up there. He walked by, and my mom told him it was terrific. I'm so proud of him.

I'm hoping to send this tomorrow as tomorrow afternoon my family leaves for the farm. Our big problem is that our car doesn't have air conditioning (if it's hot), and there is absolutely no music (tape, radio, anything). Thanks to our traveling month in July, j'ai horreur de faire mes valises. I'm so sick of doing that, I always want to pack too much. By the way, more and more I think I'll be throwing in little French phrases and words. That last one just naturally popped into my head. My mom assures me that by the end of the year, I will have lost more English than I realize. Not lost it really, but confused it, like my mom did when she was here as a young one. In French, people say, "Je prends un bain," and in English they say, "I'm taking a bath," although proper English dictates that "having a bath" is correct. Who cares, right? Plus, I'd say our group probably does it a bit anyway with our bilingualness. I still can't get out of the habit of calling commas virgules. The real challenge here is the slang, l'argot as Mme Lemire would call it. They have tons more than us, and it's usually hard to figure out what it means in context. It's worse with young people because I mostly know older people French. I'll come back saying, "J'en ai ras le bol and j'ai le trac, etc." and you won't understand me (I know those ones already. The first is a bit crude but basically means "I've had it up to here," and the other you say if you've got the jitters or something).

It's later now, and I'm off to bed soon. Like with Ashley, I'm leaving you with some quotes (you guys can share and compare, as you wish).

"To dream of the person you would like to be is to waste the person you are." Anonymous

"It's never too late to be what you might have been." George Eliot

"You can't be brave if you've only had wonderful things happen to you." Mary Tyler Moore

"The direction of our lives is more important than the speed at which we travel them." Harriet Goldhor Lern

Okay, that's enough. I hope you like them, they're fun and good to think about, and I think if you make things make sense, or fit in your own life, they can really mean something, and teach something. Anyway, I'll say my adieux and keep in touch with you à la e-mail. I LOVE YOU MUCHO (I'm so trilingual), and I'm really fine, so don't worry about me. Live happy, and remember that I think you're a beautiful, special, loving person (and that I will love you forever).

LOVE Katie BFF

P.S. – Say hi to your family for me.

SUBJECT: For Maude
SENT: 22/8/96 9:53 AM

Dear Maude (just like a letter!),

I got your e-mail this morning and of course I stashed it away in my file. (Do you know how to save mine yet?) We're on a roll. If you do manage to save it, we'll write less letters that way, which will save money for us both, and we'll become e-mail-aholics. At the moment, I'm writing you a letter, so I'm going to try not to repeat myself (even if you get that stuff later). Today, I'm going to run, then I'm going to the Palais de la Découverte with my family and some friends (family friends that is, no one really my age). That'll be so neat because they have all these inter-active, hands-on experiments and exhibits on science stuff, kind of like the planetarium, I guess. I'm happy you're happy, by the way. Did you ever know that your gid-diness reads through your letters?

As far as my family goes, I guess I'll inform you a bit. Well, my parents are happy here, but my mother is also stressed about finding work, although in reality, there probably won't be any big problem. My dad is always somewhat more relaxed in France, so that's what's up with him, whenever we see his friends and stuff. Besides that, he's trying to get some kind of contracts started, to bring in some money too. Now, me and my sister probably cause them stress though, since we don't know anything about anything where school is concerned. Everything has to wait, because Paris is full of bureaucrats (I picked that up from them). My sister "is" going to do a history course in university, but just to meet people, not so much for the course. History interests her, but she won't follow along those lines when she's back in Calgary.

I'll tell you what I know about night life, Maude, but unfortunately, without friends, I don't know much yet. First of all, Paris is totally animated at night (day too, but night is funner). There's an area here called the Latin Quarter, and I swear, I already know it almost by heart. There's always street musicians and performers out there and some of them are truly funny or good.

This wasn't at night, but one day in the metro, Christelle and I saw this guy, who came into our metro car, and sang the ly-ly-ly song by Simon and Garfunkel, and "Desperado." He was so talented, I was so proud of him, I actually had live music in the metro. We gave him a little bit of money, cause we didn't have much change, or we would have given more. It's sad though, but since there are so many beggars and poor people trying to make a buck here, Parisians have this philosophy that it's better to give nothing, or else you'd keep on giving and have nothing. I would honestly love to be rich someday, and put aside tons of money, just to go out on the streets and give it to people who need it, or deserve it. That's my dream for someday.

But the problem with Paris nightlife is that you truly need a group to do stuff with. It is not at all wise for two girls, who know nothing really, to go out alone in search of a good bar, or disco. It'll come someday, though, that's my guarantee to myself.

Unfortunately Maude, this weekend I won't be here, I'll be at my grandparents' farm. That means we can still e-mail (the computer comes everywhere with us), but calling would be pointless for you cause no one would be here. What is this thing that has been bugging you for a while? Answer if you can, when you want, I guess I can be patient. It's good for you that your sister's coming back. Say hi to her for me, kay. Whenever I write e-mail, I always feel like I jump from topic to topic, with no real link. Oh well, I'm sure you handle it.

I can't believe school starts soon for you guys. It's annoying for you guys, but it's weird for me. Say hi to people for me, if they ask about me, and say hi to Mme Lemire for me too. I love that woman.

Well, my dad wants to go back to bed, so I have to get off the computer now. If you read this in the morning, have a great day, and if you read it at night, hope you had a great day. I miss you still, but I bear with it much better now.

LOTS OF LOVE, KATIE

L.Y.L.A.S.

* * *

AUGUST 21, 1996

Dear Ashley,

I just got your letter that you sent just a couple days after our phone call. We do think alike, my dear. I kind of thought our call was a bit weird, but I don't think it reflects our relationship at all, it's totally the pressure we both feel to be ourselves, and say all there is to say. It doesn't change the fact that I know who you are, and love you. We'll get better, my dear, so don't fret.

I always have so much to say, and it's annoying cause it's so much easier to just <u>say</u> it. Anyway, remember in one of my letters where I said that it's like we're on the same wavelength all the time? I'm always so amazed cause what you write me about is usually what I'm thinking about, like finding happiness. You say you're learning how to find it, or maybe just let yourself experience it, same here. For instance, yesterday I had so much fun, and I was so happy (the day we spent with that Chris guy from Calgary and the French guys we met here). I'm learning that it is useless to hold on to negative energy and thoughts like I do sometimes, that instead I should see the positive, and thinking positive translates into a positive experience. I "knew" that before, but I'm starting to experience it, which means it actually makes sense to me now. Things you told me, like I'm in control of my emotions, and of the circumstances, that "time is of the essence" so basically not to be wasted with crap feelings, are exactly what I tell myself and try to stick to. I may come back a better person yet.

And with your sailing, it's like with Maude's work, and my coming to France. Everything, all experiences we have, benefit us, help us enjoy life, or learn something. I want to have a lot of experiences in my life to form me, to help me gain wisdom, or just a love of life and of living. Also, how you felt about the instructors and stuff, the group feeling, reminds me of how Maude feels about her work people, and how I've felt about people in my plays. It's always good to meet new people, again to open our minds, and our hearts too, so we learn to care about everyone and see some good in everyone we meet. Meeting a new person can be a life-forming experience that teaches you something, just as much as traveling somewhere new would be. I think it's so great for us to share these kinds of thoughts and opinions with each other. Like I said in my e-mail, it's almost like that's what we were meant to do for each other, to help strengthen each other's spirits. I kind of feel like the four of us are entering our journey of life together, with more awareness of the fact that we are entering it, and we're seeing what life is like more than most people our age. If we don't always agree, it's our right as individuals, but that doesn't mean we can't still love each other. I think I'm slowly learning to accept things and people as they come, and not trying to change them, but maybe just learning from them a little. I'm entering a whole new rediscovery of myself somehow, and just like you said, I still feel like you guys are a big part of it, even with the distance.

Well it's later today, and I've been organizing my letters. By the way, I was quite surprised when you said Heather thinks Brad likes me. If anything, I just think writing to each other will make us better friends, but I don't think he likes me.

Anyway, tonight we're having all the people we were with yesterday, except for Chris and the girl Kylie, over for dinner, so I peeled potatoes (you care). Tonight Mathieu and Laurent are sleeping here, and we're "seeing Paris" with them tomorrow. At least it adds a little spice to my life (jk). No, you know I'm being more positive lately, but that doesn't mean I'm about to give up my sarcasm of course.

It's later now, we had dinner, I'm in bed, and it turns out no one's staying with us. That's fine, it's calmer this way, but I now have stress because my family's going up to the beach with these people later, and I thought I'd avoided the whole bathing suit issue around guys our ages. Let me tell you, every day this week I'll be running now, and watching my fat intake, not that I'll probably stick to it, cause I never do. I could luck out, and there could be bad weather too (sounds like something really stupid when talking about beaches I know).

I wish people in France were a bit more encouraging where school is concerned. Everyone we talk to is like, "Oh, it's complete hell," etc. The last thing Chris (the hot guy from the cabin) said to me before we said bye was, "Good luck. You're gonna die." I just hope that I remember to not take the work part too seriously, because that isn't really living. Although, it's also good to keep all my options open, and things like doing well in school can open doors of opportunity, which can lead to living well. Vicious cycle, but the best thing to learn would have to be to hit a healthy balance.

Lately I feel like my thoughts are clearer. They still

sometimes don't make sense, but usually I understand more after I analyze them. If you catch what I'm saying, that's good. If not, sorry, but my clarity of thought doesn't always translate well in writing, or in speaking, even. But we both already figured out that communication is sometimes a strange obstacle to true meaning.

I hope you got my e-mail I sent before you left. Of course, you might have already been gone by the time it got there. Well, I gave you some quotes then, and as I'm still obsessed, I want to give you more.

"Life was meant to be lived, and curiosity must be kept alive. One must never, for whatever reason, turn his back on life." Eleanor Roosevelt

"Nothing in life is to be feared. It is only to be understood." Marie Curie

"No one is useless in this world who lightens the burdens of another." Charles Dickens

"When two people love each other, they don't look at each other, they look in the same direction." Ginger Rogers

"Anybody can sympathize with the sufferings of a friend, but it requires a very fine nature to sympathize with a friend's success." Oscar Wilde

"Be still when you have nothing to say; when genuine passion moves you, say what you've got to say, and say it hot." D.H. Lawrence

"I'm an idealist. I don't know where I am headed but I'm on my way!" Carl Sandburg

"Friendship is the shadow of the evening, which strengthens with the setting sun of life." Jean de la Fontaine (I saw his grave at Père Lachaise.)

Okay, I hope you didn't find that a waste of space, I just wanted to share some of the ones that I liked or reflected on the most. It's your turn now, but you have to almost be in the right mindset to appreciate those kinds of things, I think.

You know, I've decided it's really important to have connections. For instance, I'm proud cause my family has connections (people-wise) in various corners of the world, and we're welcome there anytime. That's so practical for traveling and for finding new opportunities in different places. I mean, I don't want to use people either, but it would be just as interesting to get to know people who live in different places for who they are, and it's through having an interest in meeting and finding out about people that connections automatically occur. I know I'm welcome in Mexico at Rosa's anytime, and it's a wicked opportunity, but it came naturally. So I want to seek those opportunities, like taking in exchange people, and doing stuff like that, because ties are made that way. Just thought I'd tell you, so maybe we can both seek to meet different people, and if we travel together, we can go to all corners of the world. All four of us should do it. Actually, I already have a bit of European connections for ya. I'm taking life one day at a time, but it's true that I can't wait for what's to come. I just feel so eager beaver for life!

BFF Love Katie LYLAS too
(before I forget to tell you, that means
"Love you like a sister")

SUBJECT: Welcome back Ash
SENT: 25/8/96 11:27 AM

Hi Ashley,

Well, I guess your vacation is drawing to an end now. I sympathize with you not wanting to go back to school. I know if I was there I'd feel the same way, but I also know you'll be fine when things get started. About *Remembrance*, trust me, I remember how upsetting that book was. I mean I even cried. But don't worry about finding your soul mate, it'll happen naturally, and I'll try to help you figure it out when the day comes. I kind of want to go have someone tell me about my past lives with you (remember when you wrote that in one of your letters), but I don't want it to be scary, and that book kind of worried me, but I still think I want to take the plunge. In any case, just worry about the life you're living now, it'll save you a lot of trouble.

I'm getting pretty sick of knowing nothing about school. I almost want vacation over with now, so I can know what I have to deal with. My patience is definitely running thin.

I'm at my grandparents' farm right now. You can imagine just how bored I am, plus my mom wants me to write my dissertation today (that I've been putting off for eons) and unfortunately, any mention of school work automatically puts me in a bad mood. Sucks to be me. I'm getting my hopes up though cause we're going to the beach on Thursday/Friday to see those two French guys, and at night they're going to take us to bars and stuff, with all their friends (wearing a bathing suit is still bugging me immensely). Then when we get back on the Friday night, my cousin will probably take us "en boîte," which is where you dance all night (mix between The Bank and a rave), till like 5 in the morning. That will have been my excitement for the summer, if it happens, and if it's fun.

You know I can totally see you in the future as a totally fit, active, healthy person. We can both go out to little cafés and get healthy muffins and water, then go for a night hike, or something. Wouldn't that be fun? Which reminds me, it's kind of risky of me to tell you this on e-mail, for my sake, but I'm losing weight and, of course, guess where I'm really losing it? Well, someday you may be happy to see that my capacity for cleavage is diminishing, if I keep this up anyway. My mom and my sister keep laughing at me, cause I'm so devastated, and they keep telling me I'm becoming one of them, scary thought.

Right now I'm reading *The Little Princess* again. I really want you to read it, and forget all about the movie, cause it truly sucks compared to the book. It's the kind of book that every time I read it, it gets me all emotional, and I even get chills sometimes. Frances Hodgson Burnett was such a skilled and talented writer, but you'll have to read it to see what I mean.

I'm starting to have dreams where I'm back in Calgary, after the year, and I'm thinking, oh no, I didn't appreciate it enough. It went by too fast and I didn't have fun. I think those dreams come from my fear that I'll waste this year by working too much, instead of enjoying myself. I just keep praying that everything will work out. I guess that's all I can really do though.

Maude tells me that you know that your vacation is from March 22-April 7, school vacation, that is. I guess you don't have much choice but to come then. I don't know if I'll be allowed to miss school much, but I have a while to work on my parents. I'll write again soon. Have fun, don't stress, live in the now. Enough of that, I guess. Hey, did you get my e-mail before you left for vacation, the big long one with quotes? Just tell me, I'm curious.

Okay, bye-bye, LOVE KATIE

SUBJECT: Hi Maude
SENT: 25/8/96 11:46 AM

Hi Maude,

It's me, as you know. I thought I'd let you know that I think your computer doesn't have the right date in it, cause it's a few days off. Anyway, ça va? I sent you a letter a few days ago. I hope you like it, not that it's anything exciting really. I envy you and your partying, by the way, it sure beats sitting around in a farmhouse.

Yesterday, we had a family reunion type thing, where you sit around and eat. Luckily, my cousin was as bored as my sister and I, and she took us to the city to shop and stuff. But that was depressing cause I don't think I'll ever handle this whole tight mode of fashion over here.

For your questions (the ones I remember anyway), it is important that my mom find work here. If things get really bad, and she has like nothing, our last resort was to come home and live with our grandparents. That won't happen I know, we won't even come close, but that's just to say that my mom is the big breadwinner this year. I HATE SCHOOL. Sorry, it's just building up on me not knowing anything about where I'm going, with who, in what, etc. Stupid French procrastinators, they put everything off, and leave you hanging for more than two months. You don't know how FRUSTRATING that is. I still don't know what to expect from my life here, and it's been almost 2 months! Maude, you are right now being subjected to one of my bad moods. I think I'm PMSing too, probably. That will be fun.

I'm too cranky to be writing right now, and I want you to have a good day, so do. Remember that I love you, and to enjoy your last moments of vacation.

LOVE KATIE

SUBJECT: Aaaah (Hi Ash)
SENT: 25/8/96 1:37 PM

Okay, I started my day thinking about doing my stupid dissertation, and then so that I wouldn't snack today, I ate

a full French lunch, so that now I'm stuffed to the brim
and feel so bloated! I realize you don't see my point, but
my daddy just said that this afternoon, quite soon actually, we're going to the house of friends where they have
boys our ages (as usual), and we have to bring our bathing
suits because they just built a pool, and I don't want to
swim. Life is tough. Not to mention that I only brought a
stupid bikini-type thing (with shorts, of course) to swim
with in the first place. How I am so dumb to not bring a
real bathing suit, I don't know. Well, I just wanted to share
my trivial crisis with you, as interesting as it is. Sorry I
don't have anything more exciting to say for you. Have a
nice day! (At least I won't do my dissertation now,
although my mom is mad at me now because of that.) Bye.

Mucho Love Katie

SUBJECT: Hey twin
SENT: 26/8/96 9:41 PM

Hey Heather dear,

I'm at my grandparents' farm right now, but this baby
comes everywhere with us, so I'm still able to write to
you. I wish I could retell you whatever I told you in my
other e-mail, but I don't remember a thing, sorry. Probably
wasn't too exciting, as my life isn't that exciting either.
Well, today I ran, but on country roads, and let me tell you,
it's a lot harder because the roads are so endless and the
sun is so hot. The things I do to try and get fit.

By the way, don't worry about your return to school. I
can see you now and I know you're looking gorgeous, and
you'll dazzle them all. I hear you guys had a little gathering at Maude's the other night, did you have fun? Have you
thought much about how you'll be able to drive soon?
That will be so fun for you.

Want to know what I did today? I went to a dermatologist and got my feet cut and burned again, but hey, the warts are finally leaving, so I just grin and bear it. Maybe in a few weeks I will be able to tell you I'm plantar wartless! (I know this is a dumb topic, but it'll be a big event in my life and things will be so less complicated.) Anyway, I'll send this e-mail soon I hope, so I pray that you have had a good day, and that you'll have a good start to school. Lots of love, and I miss you lots too,

LOVE KATIE

SUBJECT: A new message for you, Ash
SENT: 26/8/96 10:16 PM

Hello my dear Ashley,

I am formally responding to your prior e-mail, in hopes of communicating with you. That was so gay, it just came over me.

I started my dissertation today instead of yesterday, so at least I did something. I must admit that I hate it with an uttermost passion though, such is life, right? I was a chicken yesterday and didn't swim, I said I didn't want to, although I totally would have if there weren't people, but I think that's asking too much. When I go to the beach, on the other hand, I won't have much choice. If something happens with any guys, I assure you I'll inform you right away, but I don't think I want anything to happen cause I am sick of them. Well, not of the two guys we're going to see, but if any of their friends are as annoying as some of the guys who have tried to pick us up here, I'll vomit. (I'm exaggerating.) There could also be some great French boy, but in that case it would suck cause I'd never see him again, cause I live in Paris and not at La Baule (that's what the place here is called), so I'm not even imagining anything of that sort, but in short, it's true that you never do know, so I may have a story yet. I love how we're making so many wicked connections in this country. We have more Parisian friends now with all these insider tips and stuff they can do for us, very convenient.

I'm truly flattered that you and Lynley talked about me a little. It's nice to know that people are still thinking about me, and hey, it brings you guys closer too, so why not? I don't think you should worry about Heather and Maude, cause I know they love you as much as I do (maybe not quite as much). Everything irons itself out in time anyway, alors ne te fais pas de souci pour rien. Sorry, honestly, sometimes I just want to write in French. Strangely enough, I'm even starting to dream in French lately. It's annoying though cause although I understand more and more, I still feel like a complete dork when I speak. People here think we sound like Celine Dion, which would mean a Quebec accent, and I know I don't have that.

Are you nervous or anything about starting school again? Time does pass so quickly, you know, it's unbelievable. I really want you to read *The Little Princess*, by the way (again), it's just so inspiring. All I do lately is think, think, think about life. My thoughts are too fast for me sometimes, and I have to like tell myself to slow down. It's like my understanding is getting so much better, of things I already thought about, but that just have more meaning now.

Last night part of my dream consisted of helping [Miriam] with some problem she had, and just holding her while she cried. It seems weird for me cause I've kind of felt like her "enemy" (that's a bit harsh, but I don't know how to put it), but in my dream I felt compassion and knew that she deserved happiness as much as anyone else, and who was I to say that she wasn't good, or to judge her when I sure am not perfect! This might all seem really dumb but I felt like telling you, plus I think you understand. I want to work on that, on loving people, without all these screens of prejudice and judgments that "decide" who deserves it or not. Plus I really want to work on selfishness, not having it, that is. All this is a lifetime job, so I know it won't just happen overnight, but it's something I hope to remember whenever I feel negative.

On a lighter note, I got my plantar warts brutalized today again. But they're almost gone, so I'll live. Anyway, I'm getting weary, and I'm going to have more French dreams soon. I hope my dad lets me send this now so you'll get it during your afternoon, but if not, at least I can tell you I tried to be super speedy and great and stuff. I love you and think of you all the time (as if you didn't know).

SUBJECT: For Maude
SENT: 28/8/96 10:17 PM

Well, I'm writing twice today, it's 10 PM now and I got the message from Lyn, Kevin, Matt, and you. My mom went to Paris today and she came back to the farm and told me about the phone message. I wish I had been there to talk, it would have been so fun. . . .

Tomorrow, in the morning, my family is going to the beach, and I have to spend time with three guys and my sister, in a bathing suit. I guess I'll live though it, I hope (JK). Anyway, I just wanted to answer your e-mail and say hi again, and that I love you and miss you. Give a big hug and hi to Kevin and Matt, kay. Honestly, tell me about your classes (with who) and stuff. I hope you can stand the grade ten's, tell Terrance "Good Luck for High School" for me too. Till I get back from the beach (two days), bye-bye.

LOVE KATIE

P.S. – That means that I won't be home this weekend either, remember that. I still want you to tell me your problem though, so maybe the weekend after? If you tell me with the e-mail, we can even co-ordinate a specific day and time, so we can be sure to both be home if you want. Write back when you can, sweetie. XOXO

SUBJECT: Thanx for the message, Ash!!!!
SENT: 29/8/96 9:27 AM

Hello Ash,

I got your wicked message. I love finding out all that kind of stuff. Just so you know, this will be the last time I write for a few days, cause my family is going to the beach, and we're leaving the computer at the farm. I don't think you should worry about you know who. Don't feel bad either, you don't owe him anything. Things have changed, he definitely needs to get a grip. Don't go out of your way to make friends with him, it's not worth it. Smile every once in a while if you want, just to show that YOU have no hard feelings. But follow your instinct, which is basically that you don't care.

I think it's smart of you to try not to hate anyone (grade 10) this year, cause it's not worth your time. Hating them won't do anything, except make you bitter. Plus what do we really have to lose? (Our guys, ha, ha.)

There's tons of stress on me cause my family has to leave, but I wanted to e-mail you first. So thanx for the e-mail, don't stress about school, just go with the flow, or your instincts, and I'll get in touch soon.

Love you lots and forever and ever,

Miss you too, LOVE KATIE XOXO
P.S. – Sorry it was so short. I would have liked to have

written more, but I'll make up for it later. Have a nice day, and you smile too, just for me.

SUBJECT: I'm back!!!
SENT: 2/9/96 2:00 PM

Hi girls,

   This message is being sent to all three of you. I just want to tell you guys that I'm back from La Baule, I'm in PARIS now, and I am eagerly waiting your e-mails (hint, hint). I still have tons to hear about school, and this weekend, so get to it! (JK) I love you guys, you know that, so I guess this is it until I find out if you're checking your e-mail or not.

XOXOXOXOXOXOXO, LOVE KATIE, BYE

Expect the Unexpected

* * *

SUBJECT: Hello Ashley
SENT: 3/9/96 10:40 AM

HELLO MY DEAR,

Well, I got your message. You were quite good at recapping the weekend's events. First let me say, are you having fun? You didn't want to get involved with all that kind of stuff, but if you're enjoying yourself, don't deprive yourself. . . . I'm assuming you're still not seeing much of Maude. Are you in any of her classes? Is Heather? Is Matt? I should probably ask Maude all that, so never mind.

You're such a raving beauty, you'll probably have to deal with guys and have a boyfriend whether or not you want to. It's okay, you know, you can always chalk it up to experience, try a bit of everything. You're young, so have fun, using your good judgment and a bit of caution, of course.

I feel like I'm really starting to live in Paris now. Well, I always felt that, but now that I know you guys are in school, that all the Parisians are back, the tourists are gone, and today elementary and junior high schools started, it seems much more like the "real" Parisian lifestyle. Today when Christelle and I ran, it was super weird, cause there were a lot more people on the streets, Parisian men and women in their nice business clothes, and little Parisian children, waiting for their schools to open. I felt so foreign for the first time really. All the other times we went out, you'd see tons of tourists, little German, Italian, American families, etc., and I felt like I fit right in to the whole aspect, but now it's different.

Today my mom's calling my "school" to ask if I can start school with everyone else on the 11th, even though my exam's the 19th, and I still don't know what school they'll place me in. Such is life, right? I honestly just don't think about it. I've somewhat accepted that French people are the biggest procrastinators, you don't know anything till the last minute, plus they have a really annoying habit of automatically being opposed to everything, except if you persist, then they give in. I'll back that up with stories someday, but they're not worth writing.

It's true when you live day by day, time goes by amazingly quickly in retrospect. Ten months left, and I intend to enjoy them. Even though it might be an incredibly awkward situation, I want to hurry up and start school to get everything started. I've decided when school does start, I'm going to be like Erin, and start doing stuff with people right away, or at least try to, cause you have to spend time with people to be friends with them.

Another reason I want to make friends right away is that there might be a massive teachers' strike, which could mean a long vacation again, and I'm not about to deal with another month, or who knows how long, with just my parents. If I had friends, on the other hand, a teachers' strike would suit me just fine. Can you imagine?

That's a big problem in Paris, by the way, strikes. This country is having huge economic problems, and a lot of welfare (spend enough time with your parents and your parents' friends, you learn a lot of crap like that. I've become a regular fountain of knowledge as to the economic situations of France and Canada), and everyone wants to strike. The banks are super ticked off, and, of course, the bank we chose for our stay here is starting a strike on the 12th of September. Hopefully it won't last long. Last year there was a massive transport strike in Paris, which meant that the buses, the metro, everything stopped. The city was crippled, and there's big possibilities that it might happen again. Maybe you'll see it on the news (we did last year), and maybe I'll be in the crowd, although I strongly doubt that.

My mom is annoying me with this whole correspondence work thing. The math part is totally useless. She wants me to put all my chances on my side, which means doing well and trying to finish the math, but she doesn't understand that it isn't doing anything for me. On my last math homework, I did really well and got 15 out of 20, but I credit all of that to my dad, who pretty much had to tell me the answers. My dad won't be taking the test with me, now will he? In any case, she wants me to do math today, and I'd rather puke.

Did you read *The Little Princess* yet? Well get to it, *jeune fille*. At Maude's house, the day school started, I got another e-mail from her and Lynley, but Matt and Kevin said hi too. Kevin said he has a letter for me in the mail, and to be honest with you, I'm dying of curiosity to see what it says. First because I want to know what he's doing with his life, and also because I want to see how he writes to me. Let's just say that the last time I wrote him, I made sure to mostly just talk about my life. I didn't get mushy, or say wish you were here, or couple-ish stuff like that. I don't mind corresponding with him, if he doesn't start to call me his love and stuff. I have enough little turmoils to deal with here.

Katie and Kevin

You haven't answered me before, so I would really like to know if you are saving all these previous e-mails, or preserving them in some way at least. Reassure me that someday I'll be able to look back on this stuff, and laugh at myself, as you will, don't worry. I feel kind of bad cause my parents are the ones who have to deal with all the problems on this trip. My sister and I let them organize our lives for us, fight for our schools, and everything else, when they already have the stress of having to find work here. Yet I'm still too incompetent to do it all myself. That sucks.

Well, I hope when you read this you will be having, or have had a good day at school. I'm going to shower now, so ta-ta.

I miss you a lot, and love you forever, and ever. Your fraternal soul twin,

LOVE KATIE XOXOXOXO

SUBJECT: Hello Maude, Sept. 3
SENT: 3/9/96 9:10 PM

HELLO MAUDIE,

I always forget to take off my capslock, oh well. I got your message today, thank you, I'm proud that you wrote me before school, and don't worry, I understand that you were in a rush. You'll still have to tell me about your weekend though. I'm glad you liked the letter. I meant every word of it. Reread it whenever you want to, kay.

Well my day started out normal enough. I went running, then came home to a letter from Krista, and an e-mail from Ashley. I wrote Ashley back, showered, etc. Then after lunch my sister and I went on an excursion to find this Body Shop by our place. We got lost for a little bit, but that has nothing to do with my problem. After the Body Shop, we came home and I was in a fairly good mood. Right when my parents opened the door, they both had this ominous look on their faces, and me and my sister were both like, "What?" So my mom starts telling us how the principal of the school I wanted to go to called us today (we sent the school a letter previously), and tells my mom it's not a good idea for me to start school on the same day as everyone else, considering my exam is on the 19th, and the fact that after the exam, all could change, like my grade and even my school. On top of that, this school said they have no more room in la seconde (10th grade, the one I've decided I want to go to, since all my correspondence work showed me that I know nothing, and that skipping that year would mean severe problems when I came home, like not knowing any sciences or math), but IF I pass my test, they'd have room for me in la première (the one that is grade 11, and that I no longer want to go to). Well, despite all that, I was dealing with everything perfectly fine, cause I knew this would be the most complicated part of this trip, and I had already told myself to expect the unexpected as Ashley told me.

So there is another high school nearby, almost right next door actually, that my mom called after, and who told us to come to see them, with a letter explaining this whole complicated situation. They said the opposite of the other school: there is absolutely no room in la première, and maybe there'd be a place in la seconde. So we went like 10 minutes after I got home from the Body Shop, and were brutally rejected. Let me just say this now, to get it off my chest, BUREAUCRAT PEOPLE AND ADMINISTRATIONS ARE ALL FRIGGING BRAINLESS WITH THE COMPASSION AND INTELLIGENCE OF A FLEA. . . . PUTAIN ET MERDE!!!! (I AM GETTING USED TO FRENCH SWEARS NOW TOO). Sorry, but I was super ticked off after that encounter. The secretary brought our letter to the principal, who apparently couldn't care less, and obviously didn't read it cause she came back (the secretary) and said in this snotty attitude, "Elle dit que vous ferez mieux d'aller voir le lycée Camille Sée," the school that had already rejected me, and which, we had already clearly explained in the letter, couldn't have me. She said "oh," and turned her back on us when we reminded her of that fact, of course. WHAT A COW!!! So we left, without them saying anything else, cause they would've ignored us anyway. I'm on the brink of hating multitudes of French people because we keep meeting up with this kind of garbage, not one of them cares, and school starts in 7 days. What really sucks is that I went into that second school with a positive attitude, accepting the fact that I wouldn't be going to the other school anymore, and saying to myself that whatever happens would be meant to be, that fate would run its natural course, and everything was going to turn around. Unfortunately, all my hopes were riding on that other school, and I was crushed after.

There's like a 99% chance that the entire system of teachers in Paris will be going on a huge strike in about a week, and where will that leave me for another month? And who knows how long I'll spend knowing no one, having no friends, and when it really comes down to it, getting really bored? I'm sick of these people who put things off till the last minute. The truth is, I could end up not going to school at all if my bad luck keeps going. If no one has any room, and I fail that test, which I most probably will, cause the math is really hard, I feel like I'll be totally screwed and that they won't have anywhere to put me. What's sad though is that they won't care that they won't have anywhere to put me. They think I'm stupid cause I'm not up to their level in schooling, plus 16 is the maximum age they are obliged to make me go to school, and if they don't have to, people have told me, they just might not. You have to understand, I don't plan on being this pessimistic for long, but right now, my mind is contemplating the worst, and I can see this year come crashing down in shambles.

Actually, I already had a little crying fit and for once my family left me alone, and I already told myself to be strong, and to have faith in God cause He could still work wonders. I prayed a lot that He would make everything work out okay, so I'd have a good worthwhile year, and actually it would mean a lot to me if you would pray for me too. I feel kind of selfish, cause I know this is far from being some ultimate suffering, and other people's prayers need to be answered before this one, so for me, pray for other people who are really suffering too.

I feel weird writing all this, like you'll be disappointed in me or something when you read it. I don't want to feel bad, I assure you, I just can't help it right now. I'm sick of waiting, of everything being so unknown, and of feeling like what if this was a big mistake and my life will be forever screwed up after. But that's my super paranoia taking over, where I start to think of the impact this will have on grade 12, and graduating, and scholarships, and university, etc. I think I should slow down, cause this negative line of thinking has overwhelmed me before, and I don't feel like going through that again. I just want A LIFE!! I want to be able to go out with a group of people without being afraid of getting lost, getting raped or abducted, or assaulted. I'm sick of all my little fears here, but they're extremely hard to let go of, cause people are always leering at you, and making gross passes, and being overall scary, and I HATE IT!!!!

Don't worry about me, I still believe in all those positive things I've said, but right now, I feel pretty incapable of feeling them. In due time I guess. Maybe if I just don't think about it at all, and literally just go minute by minute, the time will just fly by to the day where I finally have a life. Until then, I'll keep hoping and praying of course, cause I love God (just felt like telling you). I love you too, and even though it felt kind of weird, it feels good to really let out my problems to a friend again, details and all. Anyway I do love you tons, and miss you just as much, and I honestly wish you were here. Oh, to have friends in the flesh again, you don't know how much I miss that. Anyway, my last attempt at goodbye, Goodbye, Sweet Dreams (I'm going to bed now).

XOXOXOXOXO LOVE KATIE

SUBJECT: Hello Heather
SENT: 4/9/96 10:01 AM

HELLO MY DEAR TWIN,

How are you? How was school today (that is if you read this after school and not before)? Thanx for telling me about your weekend, sounds like you're getting back into the whole school world. It seems strange that Brad is going to all these parties now, I don't know why though. It's not like I think there's anything wrong with that, it's just different. Do you find it weird to be in his class again?

I miss working out with you too. I often think about that Saturday night we spent at Lindsay Park pool when we swam. I had such a blast. I mean, I'm still running and stuff, but I like Lindsay Park better cause of the multitudes of options of things to do. Running can get really boring, and it's not exactly good for my knees. When (?) school starts, I'll probably have gym, so I guess I'll put in more effort this year and try to work out during gym. That way I can get fit doing other stuff besides running. Well, we'll see, you never know, I might end up not looking a whole lot different than I did before I left, but I'm trying.

You bet I brought my flannel sheets. I think I'm actually going to put them on my bed today cause I get really cold in my bed here. I'm too used to having a duvet and flannel of course. That's the only thing I really brought for my sleeping enjoyment, although I think I should have brought my teddy bear cause I always feel like I should have something in my arms before I can get to sleep. Such is life, I guess. Do say happy b-day to Andria for me, by the way.

Yesterday I found this totally great street with all these cool stores by our house, where I'll probably bring you guys when you come. So save money if you want to buy clothes and stuff here cause I assure you, it's more expensive. Maybe you'll be super lucky, and the Canadian dollar will shoot up, so you won't have to spend as much money. Oh well, that's something we can't really predict right now. You'll probably have heard from Ashley or Maude how yesterday I had super bad news about the school, and how I know nothing. I'm still pretty ticked off, but there's nothing I can do about anything, so I'll just sit tight.

Well, I'm going to go now, so again I hope you had a good day. Oh yeah, and you should be getting a letter soon. It might be boring, but what can I do? I love you forever, and miss you.

XOXOXOXO LOVE KATIE

SUBJECT: Hello Ash!!!
SENT: 4/9/96 10:33 AM

HELLO ASHLEY DEAR,
Well, I got your e-mail this morning and you definitely have a handicap for saying bye! I'm just kidding and it's not like it bothers me, quite the opposite, so don't worry. About the yearbooks, I think you should do your string pulling. If it's possible to get me one, I do believe I already paid for it, and if it's possible, please do it for Christelle too, cause it's much the same situation for her. Oh, congratulations on your running, I'm so proud of you! Maybe one day we'll both be at the same fitness level, and we'll be able to do all these sports and things together. But I have some work to do before that so don't hold your breath (I'm sure you were). I'm not printing your letters, by the way, but I do have everything saved, so I can print them later.

My dear, I'm sorry you're having complications in your life, but you have to admit it's better than nothing. Plus you know all the things you don't want to have to deal with will pass, and maybe you'll learn something in the process. I'm still surprised none of the grade tens have jumped you (figure of speech) with proposals of marriage. I'm ticked off right this second. My mom is mad at me cause I don't want to do math this minute, well kiss my butt, woman.

Sorry, she was just in here and I hate being told to do anything, cause when I'm ready and when it won't make me incredibly hostile, I'll do it myself on my own initiative. Of course no one believes me, so instead they annoy me every day by "reminding" me to do it. As to my whole situation yesterday, well I'm not quite over the angry feelings, but I promise I will be soon. I just hate thinking that it's going to screw everything up by being here, but instead I just won't think about it. I don't really feel like getting into all of that again, cause I totally said everything to Maude yesterday, and I'm sick of whining about it. Did you say Maude was crying? Was it because of what I told her, or is something wrong with her life? Tell her not to worry about me in any case, cause you're right and somehow, everything's bound to be figured out eventually. The waiting is what's really getting to me is all.

I have a big urge to go to Notre Dame today, but I doubt I will, so it was a nice thought anyway. So, are you guys spending a lot of time with Lynley lately? I hope so, but at the same time I don't (don't tell her that please). I think we could all be great friends, but I envy her involvement in the group, cause with her and without me, you guys are a foursome again. Okay, but that's just selfish paranoia, so disregard that, kay.

My mom is urging me to get ready now so I can go to the market today. I still haven't seen our market yet you see. So until later, sweetie, have a great day, and don't get stressed out with situations that aren't worth it.

I LOVE YOU SOOOOOOOOOOOOOOO MUCH!!!!!!! I MISS
YOU TOO

LOVE FOREVER KATIE

SUBJECT: Allo Maude, Sept. 5
SENT: 5/9/96 1:40 PM

Just a little hello message for you, if you get a chance to
read this before school. I LOVE YOU!!!! Thank you so much
for calling this morning, it was wicked, I do miss you a lot,
but I'm seriously okay. My sister is at the university right
now, maybe making friends for us! My parents say it's
good for you to come visit here with Ashley and Heather,
by the way. Anyway, you have to go to school (if you had
a chance to read this before school), so have a good day
(again), and don't worry about me. I love you eternally, and
am so glad we're such wicked friends.

LOVE KATIE (Remember to say hi to everyone for me.
I'm having a pretty good day now, your call was a perfect
start to it, and I had a good run.)

TALK TO YOU LATER

SUBJECT: Hola twin
SENT: 5/9/96 1:43 PM

Hello Heather,

WHAS UP CHICKIE? (RECOGNIZE?) Hi, it's me. I got
your e-mail and wanted to say gracias, it was much appre-
ciated of course. I'm doing better since that little school
crisis recently, and I'm back to my "survival" mindset.
I'm sure everything will be fine. I'm even more determined now that it will be, so it will.

I envy your religion class, I would have a blast talking
about near-death experiences. Of course, Mme Trapnell's

religion class wasn't quite like that, but hey. Did the grade
tens take over our old meeting place or not? I hear that
Daina has some recrutees, new little grade tens to join her
posse that is. Our school could turn into a big gangster
fest, and we know how horrible that would be. (Memories
of gangstas, if you catch my drift.) Anyway, I hope you
have a good day.

I love you and miss you! Till later, skater (irrepressible
urge that was).

LOVE KATIE

SUBJECT: Re: Buenos días mi amiga Katie!!!
SENT: 5/9/96 2:04 PM
TO: Ash

I was going to reply all greatly to your e-mail, and even
highlight stuff you wrote and respond to it right on the
screen (I'll do it someday so you'll understand what I
mean). But as luck would have it I'm pressed for time. . . .
I talked to Maude this morning, but you'll surely find
that out soon enough anyway. It was great. I wanted to
help you with all that psychoanalyzing stuff, but that
would be long, and so it's going to have to wait till later.
Basically, it's normal for you not to be happy all the time,
although I agree that your mind tends to cling to problems, till you feel somewhat emotionally drained or
something. Your search for simplicity is difficult, especially being surrounded by teenagerness and high school
environments. Actually I just remembered I have a
perfect quote for you, hold on. . . . "In fact, you cannot
LEAD the Simple Life; it must take you by the hand."
Janet Ashbee

There, let yourself ponder on that today, kay. Whether
or not it will have great meaning, or make sense, only you

can decide. In any case, I totally understand what you're striving for, but maybe the striving is what's making it difficult. I don't know, you tell me.

I'm sorry, I really have to go now. I'll try and write again today, I just wanted you to have something for your wake-up time. I'll reread your letter and respond to it, kay.

Adiós mi amiga, te quiero mucho!!!!!!! (another challenge for today if you don't know what that means)
BYE, talk to you later.

SUBJECT: Hello Ashley
SENT: 6/9/96 11:22 AM

HELLO DEAR ASHLEY,
Sorry, I'm not feeling very original with my subject headings. *Pippi Longstocking* is on TV right now, I'm feeling like I'm 8 again. I'm sure you care, I just felt like telling you. I'M TOTALLY SORRY TOO that I didn't get a chance to write you again yesterday, but I had no time. REFERRING BACK TO YOUR MESSAGE (shoot, I keep forgetting to take off capslock) yesterday, I'm still trying to think of something for you to call my grandma for. It's difficult, so it might take me a while, so just be patient, kay. You could always pretend you lost my phone number or something though.

Yesterday, I didn't have a bad day. I talked to Maude, ran, ate lunch with these friends of ours who came over, then later my sister and I went to this café by our house, which is near one of the high schools they might send me to. I felt like spying on the teenagers, so that's why we went. Right now all the students are going to the school to see what books they have to buy and stuff, but it hasn't started yet or anything. That's something really different about cafés in France and in Calgary. We bought one drink each (which cost us ten bucks, it's very expensive), and we stayed there for hours. We brought things to do, like work and stuff, and it wasn't a problem. They don't ever kick you out there, unlike in Calgary (some places), plus there's no limit of things you have to buy.

Today I plan on forcing my sister to come with me past the other school I could possibly go to, and see the people there. It's good cause it gives me an idea of what I need clotheswise and bagwise and stuff too. Plus there's the hope that we might strike up a conversation with some of these people, and start making friends. You never know.

My mom has decided that she's going to call acting agencies in Paris, to see if I can find acting jobs for this year. I'm not naive though, and I know nothing would come out of any of that, but again, we have nothing to lose. What could possibly be helpful is that the people who found us our apartment, our friends here, well she's an advertising person. My mom thinks she could have all these connections. More than anything else, I think this will serve to get my mind off school and stuff, just something else to think about, but if it helps, then fine.

I don't think I told you this yesterday, but my cousin e-mailed us and told us all about her trip to Portugal this summer, and she had such a blast, I'm jealous. She went dancing, bar-hopping, found all these great friends, hot guys included, and stayed up till all hours of the night. She even slept on the beach and stuff. Well, my first inclination was to be insanely jealous cause I want to be having more fun, but I'll be patient cause she told us that she has an apartment there (her dad probably gave it to her, he's Portuguese, and lives there I think). So she said she'd gladly bring us with her someday. That excites me when I need to liven up my life, so I'm already imagining going to Portugal. I know, I know, I should be concentrating on this year, but I just need something to distract me while I'm doing nothing.

You know how I said that France has only old shows here? Well they still do, but now that we have cable, I'm much more aware that they actually have tons of shows we had. Like "Sisters," "ER," "Beverly Hills," "Baywatch," everything really. By the way, I'm not going to be able to send you an e-mail every morning eventually, so don't be disappointed. You see, my dad doesn't like for us to connect very often. I'll still try, but normally, the e-mails will be there for you in the evening or the afternoon, so don't think I forgot you, but it just works better that way usually.

You know what? I'm starting to be a big lactose freak again. I'm swearing off ALL milk products right now, cause every day I have this persistent pain and it's ticking me off. But on the good side of things, I'm rapidly getting rid of my plantar warts. The last two nights were heaven for me cause I finally put my flannel sheets on my bed. It just feels so right. (I am SUCH a loser.)

I just thought, don't forget to think about me on Sept. 19th, cause that's the day of my day-long test. I hope your chem test is, or was, okay (I don't know if I can send this before you go to school). Did I already tell you that halfway through the year I might drastically change my haircut? Yup, I'm seriously considering cutting almost all of it off, but I'll tell you if it ever happens. I think you guys should buy your tickets for this spring soon, it'll be so wicked. Reassure Maude that there's room for her no problem in the apartment. It'll be so fun. Okay, I don't have much more to say, and I have to get my day rolling so, ta-ta,

BYE, I LOVE YOU AND MISS YOU ALWAYS!!!!!!!

LOVE KATIE

SUBJECT: Buenos días mi jumelle (?)
SENT: 6/9/96 10:20 PM
TO: Heather

Hi girlie,

It's nighttime here, and right now it's like 1:00 in the afternoon for you. Can you believe another weekend is just a sleep away, le temps s'écoule, what can I say? I was extremely bored today. I have a feeling I'm PMSing. (I hope your family doesn't read these.) I hope you had a wicked Friday, I wish I had been with you guys. Is that park nice? I wish I could see it. What about the braces on your teeth, are you getting them soon? Just think about how great and self-confident you'll feel when you get them off.

I sympathize with you, for your stalking of Brad. Surprisingly, for the first time, I realized that I've been there, obsessed. Of course my little obsession with him was mostly unfounded, but I can't believe I never thought of it that way before. It's like I suddenly have a slight understanding of how you could feel. Keep the faith though. It is very possible to get over him, I'm proof of that. I don't want to make you think about it too much though, cause Maude told me you prefer to not think about it. I totally understand, but if you ever want to have a break-down about it, I'm here, just a keyboard away (I'M A LOSER). Honestly, I do feel like our twin experiences, the fact that I've partially been there (I am aware that our relationships with him were quite different though) will help you, maybe. We'll see, plus you could always bump into some hot guy at a rave or something someday soon, and "poof," Brad will be gone forever.

Wow, I'm skilled at not talking too much about something I said I wouldn't talk about. Oh yeah! You guys are getting out at 2:15 today, I completely forgot. Heather, I am DYING (said in a dying kind of voice) to meet people here. I feel like I'm getting family fever or something (get it, like cabin fever, except you say family instead . . . okay, I'll shut up now). I'm teetering on the brink of insanity, and if I don't meet teenagers, not slimy gross guys, but nice, funny, friendly people who could make friends for the year, I'll fall into the ever consuming catacombs of craziness. (I hope you realize that was all a dramatic effect I was striving for, with alliterations and everything. Yes, I am THAT bored, Heather.) HA, HA, HA, HA, HA, HA!!!!!! That did it, I'm crazy.

I hope I'm entertaining you, cause I'm entertaining myself . . .

I have nails now, I have forgotten to tell all you guys that for the longest time, I keep forgetting, such is my memory. They're really quite lovely, and I feel oh-so-feminine now. I could also gouge people's eyes out if need be. When I'm super bored, I try to be a drummer, and tap my nails to different beats. If I get nothing else out of this year, I'll learn to tap my nails rhythmically!! Hee, hee, I truly think I'm a dumb girl, or maybe not.

Please save or print this message after you've read it, so someday I can read it too, and recall this momentous occasion in my life. I want to be able to show my kids someday and say, "Look, sweetie, mommy lived in Paris and for a little while, was bored out of her mind, but she's perfectly sane now. And look how funny she was!!" And then I'd break out into fits of maniacal laughter and start rolling on the ground, tears from my demented laughter coming out of my eyes, my kids' screams mixed with my psychotic laughter. Whoa, that was scary, wasn't it? When the mind lives in boredom, it naturally turns to the imagination, which takes over, and makes up stuff like that, which make no sense, and in no way reflects the mature,

SOUTH CENTRAL REGIONAL LIBRARY

responsible, clear-minded, and perfectly sane person that I am.

No really, Heather, this is all in jest. Sadly enough I'm getting my little kicks out of writing all this. I'm fine, just having a little bout with boredom (YES!!!! ANOTHER ALLITERATION).

I have a feeling I'd be really ashamed of all this if I read it in another state of mind, so I won't. I will send it to you without looking back. . . . I really think I'll go now, I do kind of want you to save this though, can you? À un de ces quatre, ma biche, grosses bises, je t'embrasse fort! (translation, till later my dear, and the rest basically means I LOVE YOU.)

LOVE KATARINA, KATIE, KATHERINE, KATE
(the different names I've acquired throughout
the years from various people)

SUBJECT: Bonjour Ashley!!
SENT: 7/9/96 10:16 PM

Hello Ashley,

So how is your Saturday going? Mine was fine, nothing big to tell you, but it was fine anyway. No really, what did you do today? It can amuse me to imagine what you guys are doing during the day, like when I know you guys have lunch, I think about how the posse splits up, and where the different cliques go. If I was really bored, I could even imagine dialogue between you guys, but that's pretty sad, and I'm happy to say I haven't been there yet.

I really wish you were feeling happier, I honestly do. I wish I had some magical advice, or some way to get you out of your slumps. I'm thinking maybe you have to start an extracurricular activity. I was thinking how Maude and I have both had good experiences with that kind of thing, getting involved in a group out of school that takes our mind off school and is an enjoyable learning experience in itself. I know if I was there this year, I'd be throwing myself into that kind of stuff, even something that only takes a day a week. I know you might not think you're the type of person to join a group thing without anyone, but you have to start somewhere. Don't even do it with anyone else from school. Find something that is of interest to you, that can become YOUR world, and that can maybe add some new perspectives to your life. I think that's really important, to meet new people without the help of anyone else, and form alliances out of school, but you have to be willing to take

Katie (second from left) at University of Calgary summer hiking camp, 1995. Ashley under the hiking bag.

LOVE YA LIKE A SISTER

the plunge and take the risk that you might not love it. If you don't, and the people aren't great, at least you tried, and maybe you got something out of it. I think you could start to feel more self-confidence if you did something like that by yourself, and could say to yourself, "I did it and it wasn't that bad." I truly believe doing my plays brought me more self-confidence, and made me meet people I wouldn't have otherwise, and like they say, each new person we meet or befriend represents a new world in us.

If this idea appeals to you, drop piano or something, and start looking through program things, with University of Calgary, or the Y, or anything you can find. If I could, I would take at least ten programs my mom found here to learn something new that actually interests me, like learning massage and yoga, and, above all, to meet more people. Connections and contacts with many people can help you out a lot of the time in the long run. Just think, I know someone who is maybe getting a job as a flight attendant (traveling!) because of a friend's mom or something like that. "The wise man makes more opportunities than he finds." Sorry, I had to add that and I forget who the author is, and I'm too lazy to look. I memorized that, isn't it good!

I'm honestly wondering, do you realize how quickly time flies? This year seems like it will pass by in a flash, except it doesn't feel that way at the super boring times, but you know what I mean. Grade ten went by in a flash too and, before you know it, we'll graduate, then have to be big girls. Wow, see, when I start to think like that, I really start telling myself to enjoy my youth, cause it won't last that long, and I would hate to look back and say, "what if, I wish I had . . ." so I'd like it if some friends came out of the woodwork right about now so I can start enjoying myself this year! This year is definitely starting out as a trial of my patience, that's for sure. It reassures me though to know that the first six months my mom was in Paris the year she met my dad, she hated it and she was totally depressed, then she met people, mainly my dad, and she enjoyed herself. I don't think my bad times will last 6 months, not even close, so I'll be fine.

I don't know how to tell Lynley and Maude this, but Christmas is not exactly a time when people could come. I wish it was, but the truth is my family says we're going to be in Raindron at my grandparents' most of the time, and it would still be possible to have one person come, but only one cause our car wouldn't have room to take two (it's VERY small, not the rented van we had in July). So if anything, it might be super boring, although I have to admit we don't know anything about the exact dates we'd be going up to the farm, so we might spend a lot of time in Paris in the end. It's just not likely, and I'd hate it if people didn't have a good time, or get to do the things they really wanted to do. Plus it's a lot to get organized before then, it's getting close. Overall, it kind of scares me cause I don't want to disappoint anyone. If Lynley wanted to come, she'd really have to be alone, and she'd have to get organized quick. I don't know why I told you all that, maybe just to enlighten you, so you can break it to them. (Hee, hee, hee, I'm sorry, I'm a cruel girl.) I'm not saying Lynley can't come, but it takes some planning and some willingness on her part to spend some time, maybe a lot (?) at my grandparents. So that's the scoop. Tell Maude I'm sorry, or actually I can tell her myself, but can you just tell her the whole deal cause I think it's something that is easier explained in words, than typing. Plus I'm too lazy to do another e-mail tonight, and I'm sure you'll get to tell her before I do anyway. (The truth comes out.)

So, I don't know what you'll be doing when you read this, but I hope you have a wee smile on your face, cause smiling can change the way you feel, from bad to good. I told you to have sweety dreams last night (that seems so time dysfunctional, cause it wasn't my last night but yours, ANYWAY . . .) so sweet dreams again for when you sleep later on. I WAS SO glad to hear your voice, by the way. I love it when I'm transported back to Calgary, and of course, I LOVE YOU!!!!!!!! Even oceans away, as my fraternal soul twin, we seem to be feeling the same things, maybe for different reasons, but you know that recently I haven't been all happy-go-lucky. I'm not feeling really bad or anything, but boredom can make anyone a bit bitter. So I'm saying bye-bye now, and I'm going to make up dreams about someone, a French someone of course, ooh, I can't wait.

Ta-ta my dear, be happy, remember that I love and miss you, and think about how someday you'll be a bridesmaid at my wedding, and hopefully a godmother to one of my children (?). I don't know where that came from, or why it came, but it did, so you can imagine it anyway.

Love your forever fraternal soul twin,

LOVE ME, XOXOXOXOXOXOXOXOXOXOXOXOXOXOXO (look how special you are)

SUBJECT: Hello Ashley
SENT: 8/9/96 10:04 PM

Hi my dearest Ashley,

Well it's Sunday night as I'm writing this to you, and I've had a very good day, but I'll tell you about that after cause I have some urgent business on hand to inform you of. We just got a phone call from my grandma in Calgary, informing us that the city plans on expanding 14th Street to ten lanes. Which would mean the destruction of my home, my grandma's home, Kent's home, our whole community would be torn apart!!!!!!!! You have no idea how much I want to be home right now so I can help save it. Apparently one of our neighbors that we babysit for is already starting a committee to organize strategy, or something. You might have already known this, but I had to tell you anyway. They might take away my home!!! I will hate the mayor if he does this, and I've loved him up till now. You have to admit that I have a wicked community, it's so nice and civilized, friendly and old-fashioned. I mean we still have block parties! Everyone's friends with everyone, and it's so many families' true homes, you know.

So, in light of this tragedy, I'm asking you to help, since I can't (I would honestly go and talk to the mayor myself if I had to). Now, I know it might seem like there's nothing for you to do, which I understand, which is why I realized this could also be an incredibly good reason to call my grandma, and tell her I told you about our problem, asked you to help, and how you love my home as your second home too, so you want to help (RIGHT?). On top of that, my grandma is in charge of going around collecting names for a petition, so you can ask her if you can help her. Not only is it a perfect way to keep in touch with her, but she will love you even more for the offer and the help. Plus, if you dragged our friends into helping, that would rule. Just remind them that they love my house (?) so they want to save it too, or something. I'm sorry if this seems unfair of me to ask you to do this, but please, I have to feel like I can still do something, even if that means just enlisting more help.

So you've heard my crisis, seriously consider it. You could become Ashley the Activist, and everyone would admire you for fighting for a good cause. Plus they only want more lanes so big pollutant trucks can go on it. I hate big pollutant ****ing trucks (my little censorship, ha, ha,)

I'll keep writing after dinner, Bye-bye.

SUBJECT: It's me again!!
SENT: 8/9/96 11:02 PM

Hi,

I just thought when I kept writing after dinner it would be fun to make it a whole new message. I bet it's just a blast for you. You know, my family's dinner conversations never cease to amaze me with their utter stupidity sometimes. Oh well, it's amusing, plus I like contradicting my dad. I think I'm a good debater. Anyway, so I won't talk about my devastating news about my home anymore, I'll tell you about my day. I think I encouraged you enough to help in my last message anyway.

So, I started my day with a pretty crappy run, cause I got cramps similar to the tummy ache I got going back to Andria's that time. I know you know what I'm talking about, all I have to say to remind you is tree. That feeling is in part due to the fact that I'm a big lactose freak again, I can't even take butter recently. Well, that sucks big time and it also means that for the past week I've been mega bloated, and you know the rest. Then when I was doing my weights and stuff, I pulled some back muscle and it still hurts, but at the time it was spasmic, and I couldn't stand straight. In consequence, all day I have felt bloated and my back has been really screwy. I swear I just lived the day in the life of a pregnant woman. My stomach was out and my back was curved, you see, and there was nothing I could do to change that, but it was fun sometimes to imagine that I was pregnant and that my husband was taking care of me and stuff. But that's because I'm a pretty dorky girl that I was thinking all that.

ANYWAY . . . so after lunch my family went to this really big famous museum here, and looked at all this art. It was really neat, and there were some paintings I wish I could buy. As if, of course. Cause it would cost gazillions and they wouldn't sell it anyway. So then after that we came home and waited for our neighbors (the ones with the young daughter Mathilde, who invited us over once). It was fun, and their other older daughter came too, it felt all animated. As a result, my sister and I are going to go out with Mathilde tomorrow, maybe to a movie, or just exploring, but we're getting to be actual friends, and she has so many connections for us, I can't wait. Plus she's so nice, and it will be nice to go out not just the two of us, and without the parents for a change. In any case, I kept busy today, so I didn't mope at all, and I had a good time, and of course this day passed in a flash, so now I'm going to start a whole new week again. Nifty, huh?

Anyway, my poor mommy is exhausted and wants to go to bed, so I'll let her by getting out of her room, and off the computer. Have a nice day, or night, and definitely have a happy Monday if I don't communicate with you before then, kay. Put a smile on your face, and don't create problems for yourself. Like I said, just go where life takes you and try not to question too much. Consider that whole saving my neighborhood thing, cause I would appreciate it SOOOOOOOOOO much. I love you lots, and miss you tons,

Adiós mi amiga, Te quiero mucho XOXOXOXOXOOXXO-OXOX

LOVE KATIE

There's So Much I Want to Know

* * *

SUBJECT: Buenos días mi amiga
SENT: 9/9/96 9:10 AM

So Ashley,

It is Monday morning for me and I just read the e-mail you sent last night, with your mommy saying hi. You know what's ironic? Before I even read your e-mail today, my mom said, "Tell Ashley I say hi," and then your mom said hi to me. Strange, huh? This next little paragraph is for your mom.

Hi Ashley's mom, I'm sorry Ashley isn't telling you all about Paris, so I should tell you that everything is fine. We still have to meet people here, and to start school, so for now it's still like we're just on a vacation here. Everything fell into place where my parents finding work is concerned. My mom already has several conferences lined up now, and my dad still works with Calgary and Colombia (with his computer, of course), and he might have some contracts for here. I hope Ashley gets organized to get the plane tickets. I'm sure you're trying to motivate her, but I know that can be a difficult thing. In the meantime I'm waiting for school to start. Paris is alive with people now that all the Parisians are back from holidays. It's definitely an animated city. We've done a lot of visiting, to museums, monuments, and just things that interest us. We were really lucky for our apartment, it's great, and it's only a 20 minute walk from the Eiffel Tower. So everything is good here, and thanx for asking. I hope in the future Ashley will inform you too. Bye, Katie

Now back to you, Ash, how did this Monday go? I really can't wait to go out with our neighbor today.

I will seriously consider helping out about the 14th Street situation, but I will feel kind of retarded but hey, I've never done it before.

See, that's a highlight. I move your words from your e-mail into my e-mail so I can make comments. It's like we're having a conversation, almost. I want to say, if you feel retarded about helping, get Heather or someone to do it with you. I'm desperate, and I know you'll come to the right decision.

Oh, Ash, you really should get organized with the whole ticket deal, but is Maude coming with you guys, or not? If she's lazy, force her, cause it will actually be better for you guys if all three of you come. First, because when I can't be with you guys, three people is always better than two to feel safe taking the metro and stuff (not that it's dangerous or anything though). Plus for sleeping here, it makes everything work better actually, cause I think I can only fit one person in my room, and we have a pull-out bed for two people, but I know you or Heather might feel awkward sleeping out on it alone, so if there were two there, two in my room, we could alternate and stuff, you see. Anyway, try to convince Maude, that is if you want her too (JK). Now, I'm going to respond to stuff in Bonjour Katie, and use wicked highlighting techniques.

Lately I have been thinking about how there is so much I want to know in my life, I am scared I will never get the chance. Also, for some reason, I have this strange idea in my head that I need to go to Ireland one day. I don't know why, but I feel like something is there for me, but when it comes to my strange feelings, I don't know how much I trust myself. I don't know if it is just a strong will or desire to go there that I made up, or if something is really there for me. Oh well, I guess I'll have to go and find out.

Well, first of all, like I've told you before, it's strange how we both think of the same things, even oceans away. I have also been thinking about how there's so much I want to know, to learn in my life, and it honestly seems too short for everything. Like with my library here, I look at all the different sections and all the books, and I honestly could read every one, or almost, there's so much that interests me. But I don't just want to know book stuff, I want to know how to do things, and how to be different. Because of this feeling I always hate feeling like I wasted a day just watching TV or something, although that can be beneficial sometimes. I hate it when I feel like I could have done something that day that would have been more worth my while.

As for Ireland, well if you want to go there, I'm ready and willing to accompany you. We could do this big trip and visit that guy in Wales that I met this year, and then move on to Ireland. I have always had a big desire to see it.

I don't think I've ever considered that there is something there for me, but I have thought that it's something I really have to see someday, especially with the Garth Brooks song "Ireland" that I love so much.

You know, we could drop by Scotland while we're at it, cause there I do feel like I have to go, it's a part of my origins, and I really loved *Braveheart*, so I'm super proud of Scottish people now. I could go there and research my family's history, even though I already have it. Did you hear about how they recently found Braveheart's heart? Yup, after he died, I don't remember who, but they cut it out, and it has traveled all over Europe, and disappeared for a while, but now they found it again. I think that is so neat.

I can't wait to do all kinds of traveling in my life. You know what's important though, to stay with families and stuff where you go, because it's true that otherwise you don't really get to witness the culture, which is more interesting to me than hotels and typical tourist stuff. It's better to have insiders tell you what to see and where to go. It can have so much more meaning. We merely have to get connections in all those places.

Wouldn't that be weird if your little boy and my little girl, or vice versa, got married? That would be such a great event for our old age, don't you think?

You know what, I've thought about that too. It would be so neat if we shared grandchildren and stuff, we would totally spoil them. I agree that we can't bring them up as brothers and sisters, but I think it's okay if my kids call you Auntie Ashley anyway, cause kids are kids and if they play together and stuff, and later on they understand that they're not blood related, then they'll have their own minds to rely on. I'm trying to say that despite what happens when they're kids, when they're teenagers they will either like each other or they won't. If anything, at least they can just be great friends, Maude's kids and Heather's kids too. Actually it's strange, cause I can imagine me, you, and Maude with our little families, but not Heather. I'm not sure if she's ever told me that she wants one. She could be little bachelorette if she wants, we'll still love her.

I just got the thought that the reason I have not been all that happy lately is that I am supposed to be doing something, but I am not fulfilling whatever I have to do.

That's why you must do something, like your sailing to feel productive. Ski racing sounds good. Skydive, or bungee, or I don't know, I'm just trying to be helpful. I'm completely aware of that feeling though. Then I remind myself that I'm putting all this pressure on myself, and I just have to try and accept whatever I have at the moment, or do something to make me feel like I'm accomplishing some purpose. Volunteering is always good, cause it can be fun, and you feel good about doing something helpful for free, and helping people in this world, I think, is our ultimate duty, or something. So think about all that. Well, I think this is a pretty long e-mail, so I'm going to go now. Hope you had a terrific Monday, and found something good in the day.

À demain mon amour, ma chère amie, (we are so trilingual, n'est-ce pas?)

BYE, LOVE YO (think Spanish)

XOXOXOXOXOXOXOXOXOXOXOXOXO, infinite (beat that)

SUBJECT: Hi Ashley
SENT: 10/9/96 9:59 AM

Hey Ashley,

Yes, I know my title is simple and plain, but that's life when you're lacking originality. So, I got your e-mail this morning, thanks, it was great. I'm going to tell you all about my day yesterday, then I'll answer your stuff, kay. So, we had a really good time yesterday. During the day I didn't do much, except I used my sister's big *Supple Body* book to find stretches for my back. I felt very frustrated because of the whole pregnant feeling issue without having an apparent reason for it, but now I'm okay because I got "my little friend" you know, so I have an excuse. And besides that, I watched zillions of music videos, went to the Poste to send a letter to Krista and to Andria (writing them back). My whole day was revolving around going out at night.

So, our neighbor Mathilde came over at 6 or so, and we walked to this little cinema place nearby, and stood in line for a while. Then the people who worked there announced that they weren't showing the show we were waiting for. It was actually a premiere to another movie that won in the Cannes film festival, and the director was going to be there too, but we'd have to wait an hour and a half, so we decided to move on. We walked to this area nearby that's swimming with movie theaters and found ours. So we went in and watched the movie, it's a French one so you won't know it. It was pretty strange, and I thought a bit pointless, but most French movies have no plots, so I dealt with it.

So after the movie we decided to go to a café and get a drink. I finally got an alcoholic beverage at a café, cause I asked what was good (no beer for me). So we sat there, talking for a long time. It was good cause we started talking about our lives, not just crap. Before that we had a pretty good talk, like we weren't awkward or anything, but it was not stuff that ends up bonding people. So, this was better, and retarded as I am, I felt tipsy leaving.

We took the metro back to "our" places, and she went to her place but told us to call in half an hour, and that way she would see if her friends were doing anything, and if they were, we could go too. But, at our door, we realized we didn't have our keys, so we had to go to Mathilde's since we had nowhere else to go. Surprisingly, we saw that our parents were over there too. Well, we didn't end up going anywhere else that night, but we ate dinner at Mathilde's with her family and stuff, and it was good.

So, it's not like it was exciting, but I truly felt like I was living in Paris for some reason. Plus, we're getting better at communicating, so in high school I think I'll be okay. It's neat to have good neighbors, that will help us if we have no keys, etc. I really have no idea how to explain this feeling, but I don't feel like I'm on vacation anymore. You know what, if I was starting school tomorrow, I might have been so stressed today. I'm not, so hey.

Now, that was my night, and we'll probably be doing more with her this week, cause she said she's going to show us the good bus routes, good cafés, stores, and maybe we can go to parties and gatherings with her.

Just think, when we are married and hopefully well off, 'the girls' can go to a place on vacation without the rest of the family. Won't that be fun!!!! We could go like once every two or so years, and maybe our hopefully gorgeous beaux can join us a few times too.

Good idea, but I think it would also be good to do a lot of traveling alone before we're married. I know that poses a money problem, but what if we went after we were married, we'd have all these problems turning down all the guys in all the countries. I saw a movie that was exactly that story almost. She had an affair when she went to Rome with her friends, so maybe we should do a lot of exploring before because then we'd be free, to try a little of every country (hee, hee). Of course I still want to travel with you after we're married, and there actually shouldn't be any problems if I love my husband more than anything. I guess I'm just saying that I'm scared I'll go somewhere and realize that some person I meet is actually the true love of my life, but it's too late to do something about it cause I'd be married. I'm just being paranoid, but I don't want to ever have that problem, talk about stress. It's going to be so hard for me to find someone to marry cause I think I'll always question, "Is there someone I love more in this world, who is actually meant for me, and am I about to make the biggest mistake of my life?" Oh-oh. Well, we'll have to help each other with opinions on the men in our lives, so we can save each other from a bad decision, whether that means letting someone go, or taking the plunge, we'll have to see. Life's not simple, is it?

Owie!!!! My foot's asleep and now I have pins and needles. That sucks. As for the Braveheart heart, I don't remember how it was preserved, but it was somehow, but it's not like it's still bloody and soft, more like hard and black. Did you know that Celine Dion is afraid she might lose her voice, permanently? To try and save her voice she barely talks when she's on tour and stuff, but usually writes everything she has to say. That's a life lived in fear.

Anyway, I must be going now, hopefully for a run, so I'll talk to you soon my dear. Have a good Tuesday, or hope you have had a good Tuesday. I'll do my best to have a great one here. Adiós mi amiga favorita,

XOXOXOXOXOXOXOXOXOXOOXOXOXOXOOXO <Gazillion times infinite (We are so cool, Ashley)

Love, me

SUBJECT: Hi my twin!
SENT: 10/9/96 10:17 PM
TO: Heather

Hello there girlie,

Well, this is the first e-mail I've sent since my little insane one. Did you get that one? Anyway, it's nighttime, and I'm doing nothing, therefore it's a choice opportunity for me to write you. I must inform you that today I got your letter, it was great! You know what I think is really true, finding out who your true friends are. They're the ones that visit you in prison, or in the hospital, and who write you when you move.

ANYWAY, I just finished reading this really good book (yes, in French), but it was super psychological and, for some reason, I now feel all foggy. Have you ever read a really good book, that just got you thinking and questioning things, and almost leaves you disturbed when you're done cause it's so real? I have. I think we should start a book club someday, and get people to read the books we like, or even the ones we hate, so we can have healthy, heated discussions on them. I love books, really, I know that is typically a "geeky" thing to say, cause reading has all these brainy, which is considered dorky, connotations attached to it, but I admit it. "Read. Not just what you have to read for class or work, but to learn from the wisdom and joys and mistakes of others. No time is ever wasted if you have a book along as a companion." There you go, I didn't memorize that if you were wondering. I pulled it out of my dandy quote book in fact.

I'm positive I've asked you this before, but it's a pertinent question since you still haven't answered me. Are you saving my e-mails? Please do, or at least print them, for my own memory, and because, unless you want me to do it the traditional way, these are our letters now. Sorry, if that bugs you let me know, but it's a lot easier and cheaper that way. Tell me if you think otherwise.

By the way, I loved your drawings in the letter!! They were so talented, and I still feel so guilty cause I never gave you a picture for your wall. You have to understand that I need to be moved to do that, and I can't just draw anything. You'll have to wait till the day when I find something worthy enough for your wall that is good enough for you, and that I can put real effort into. In the meantime, you know that I love you, despite my lack of art. Speaking of walls (what a practical transition), I think your painting idea is a good one. Yellow is bright and happy, and blue too, and you should have a positive room. Wow, that is such a fun idea, I think I'm forming an idea for what I'm eventually going to make you for your room. When I get back, I'm going to help you make a positive room. You'll have to hold me to that promise, as I might forget, alrighty?

Well, my dad is kicking me off the computer, so adiós for now. I hope you had a great Tuesday, and remember that if you didn't, there's a brand new day just waiting to unfold.

LOVE YOU FOREVER, ALWAYS AND TOUJOURS, SMILE TWIN!!!

LOVE KATIE

SUBJECT: Hello Maude Sept. 11
SENT: 11/9/96 11:03 AM

Hi Maude,

It's great to have you back among the land of the e-mailers. I am such a dork. Oh well, so last night I got your first message, but as you guessed it, I didn't have a chance to write you back. So, this morning I had it all planned out to write, and I got another one from you!!!

When you read this it will be Wednesday for you, and I hope you'll be feeling better than you were yesterday. Don't be confused by what I'm about to do, it's called highlighting, and it makes it so we're almost having a conversation, cause I respond to stuff you said. If you're still confused, ask Ashley.

Not to sound depressing or anything but right now I'm really missing you, more than other times. Maybe cause right now I'm listening to "Wind Beneath My Wings," and it's in that movie, *Beaches*, where that lady dies, and I know that you aren't dead, but you aren't here, and it's just kind of depressing. Imagine if you did die while you were in France. That would be so incredibly bad cause I never really got the chance to say bye and it would be so scary. Then I wouldn't know what to do. Would your funeral be in France or here in Canada? Oh, Katie, please don't die on me now cause then it would make my life so ugly and I wouldn't be able to go on with my life, and then I would become a complete failure depending on welfare. So what's new with the school?

I promise I won't die when I'm here, I have way too much to do in my life to die this year. I don't know how come I'm so confident, but I am. I totally know that I won't die, God wouldn't let me, so don't worry your pretty little head. Oh, I don't think you must have noticed, but yesterday wasn't August 10, my dear, more like Sept. 10, but don't worry, my e-mails are arranged in order so I know. Look, I'm racking my brain for the homework poem you asked me to think up about our era, but I honestly don't have a clue. I actually don't think I truly understand what an era is, so I'm horribly sorry, cause if it had been about the sea, or love, or something like that, I would have maybe.

About school, well, to be honest with you, nothing's new, but I'm fine, just so you know. If I had started school with everyone else, which is today, I wouldn't have been able to write you, now would I? Plus, I think maybe it was the best choice for me, although I couldn't accept it at the time, but it might have just made me more screwed up to start like that, in a school and a grade where I might not really end up. So, like I said, I just accepted it, and I'm avoiding thinking about school for the moment, cause the day of the test (scary) is approaching. My sister, on the other hand, has been officially accepted into university, but she isn't starting till October 7. So we are learning to become patient beings, and all is well.

Actually, I don't feel like retelling it all, so you can just ask Ashley, but we went out with my neighbor the other night, and it was good. I felt like I was really living in Paris, with other Parisians, for some inexplicable reason. I'm forever learning that God knows what He's doing, and you really just have to keep the faith (as you saw, it's not always easy, but hey, that's life). My mom has also got several more conferences lined up already, and I think that's great cause she hasn't even worked once yet. Like the people still don't know what she's capable of, so when they do, she'll be rolling in the dough.

I'm so glad that you guys are getting your tickets now. I mean I've known people were coming, but I don't think I would totally rely on it until I knew the tickets were bought. Don't worry about being unwanted or anything, you're perfectly welcome, and we do have the room. Plus, like I explained to Ashley, it actually is better this way, cause it evens stuff out, and yet again I'm too lazy to repeat it, so you can ask Ashley if you want details on what I mean. In short, je suis ravie que tu viennes! Our little foursome will be all reunited again, it'll be so fun! When you for sure know details, like dates, times, airports, stuff like that, tell us cause it's good to get all that organized as soon as possible. No anxiety that way. Try not to pack too much in your suitcases, cause we really do have a small car, but actually don't worry about that yet, it can wait.

Today while I was in the chapel meditating in religion, I thought about you the whole time and tried my best to ask God for you to have a good time and that you adjust and get into your school easily. So good luck, sweet cheeks, and remember to try to keep on smiling.

Thanks Maude, that means a lot to me. I don't want you to worry about my happiness because I truly am happy, and peaceful. I think it will happen, I really just have to learn patience. You know. I pray for you too, and that's because despite the distance, I still love you to death! I'm sorry you're feeling so whatever about life, but it's good that you're thinking of getting really involved and stuff. That can always be beneficial, just don't get in over your head, because then you'd be stressed, and it wouldn't be worth it. I think you should really try for your license, let me be your motivator. You can do it, Maude, just take it slowly, and you'll get it before you know. All you have to do (if you're doing this) is call the Alberta Motor Association and book 5 classes. It's not difficult, and it really doesn't take up much time. I guarantee it will give you freedom, you will totally appreciate it, and the minimum time you have to spend is 10 hours, but you have to be as determined as I was, kay?

Look, I would write more but my mom wants me to go buy a baguette for lunch, so I have to get off. I hope you have a great day, and remember, I'm not going to die, and you better not either!!!!!!!

I love you to death, always, XOXOXOXOXOXOXOXOXOX-OXOXO

Love Katie

SUBJECT: Hello Ashley
SENT: 11/9/96 12:36 PM

Hello Ashley,

I hear from Maude that you guys are getting your plane tickets today, good for you!!! I'm proud of your decisiveness. Don't forget to inform me though on all the specific details that are implied, like times, etc. Normally, I would be at school right now, but I'm glad I'm not, first because it's still a stressful situation, and second because I would look all bloated and gross for my first impression. At least this way, I have more time to look good before I go. I do want them to have a good impression of Canada, such a wonderful country that it is.

Yesterday, I went to the library and took out some books. I can't believe how archaic their system is!! They have all these rows of books they class under "roman," which basically means all stories that we would have classed under mystery, romance, fiction, etc., but all of theirs are arranged alphabetically according to the author. Let's just say it's not easy to actually find a book you want to read. You have to read all the back covers and it's a very stupid process. Plus, do you remember how we took out books in elementary with Mme Wilshire, well, they do the same thing. They have little cards in all the books, where they stamp on it. It's SOOOOO ancient. And to think this is a city library, like the one for our whole district, that's a mighty sad thing. Oh well, books are books, and it's still possible to find good ones, cause I managed, and I already finished one. It was really good for some reason, and I think you'd like it (it's originally an English book). It's all psychoanalytic, like we like them, and it has to do with teenagers.

Well, I'm dreadfully sorry that the hockey game finished the way it did. I could see you were devastated. Don't let it get to you though, that would suck. Last night I saw a made for TV movie about a man who left his wife for another woman, and the wife went crazy and killed both of them. It's normally American, with actors you would recognize (don't remember their names), and it really got to me. I guess cause it was a true story, and I felt for all of the people involved. They had four children, and she got so bitter, it made her crazy. I thought it was so sad that she killed her spirit the way she did, cause she let the bitterness take over her entire life, and ruin everything she could have kept despite the divorce. I honestly felt like her soul should have been nurtured, and it was so sad that she'd never been able to live her life without her husband. He became her life, and she didn't exist to herself anymore. I don't know why I'm telling you all this except that it seriously disturbed me. Plus, the story reminded me a lot of friends of my parents that had a divorce, and I suddenly realized how incredibly difficult and horrible it must have been for the wife. I think, to a smaller extent, I understand the husband, but their story hasn't taken a psycho turn, and he didn't have to deal with what the man in the movie did, so I can't sympathize with his side. Overall, I think it's the saddest thing for a marriage to break up, especially if one is totally against it, because they promised together to spend their lives together, to live as one, and then all of a sudden, one of them gets replaced, new life, new wife, and where does that leave the person who had fixed in her mind that she would live out the rest of her days with that one person? Frighteningly lost, if you ask me. It scares me almost, cause I don't know if I could endure something like that, and when you give your trust so completely, by marrying someone, it would sure be difficult to ever regain trust for anyone, after having been so brutally betrayed.

I'm going to have lunch now, so have a good day and be happy for me, cause you deserve it, sweet cheeks (Maude expression). Don't think too hard about anything, especially if it's upsetting you, just focus on enjoying living. Okay, enough Katie advice,

Adiós mi amiga, buenos días,

Love you forever always, Love Katie
XOXOXOXOXOXOXOX
XOOXOXOXOXOXOXO
(all the XO's on heaven and earth)

SUBJECT: Hola Ashley
SENT: 12/9/96 10:30 AM

Dear Ashley,

Today my mom got the paper that says I'm signed up for that test, it's SOOOOOOO scary. Plus we just discovered that I have to take a test on Spanish too, so I'm cracking the books today. I think I'm going to start taking this test a little more seriously, cause if I know nothing on the day of the test, I might break down there, and that would be mucho embarrassing. Guess what Brad told me? Gym is his favorite class cause he finds you so entertaining, and your stories are the funniest. You're a special girl, you are.

Well, I have mounds to do today, so I apologize too for the shortness of this e-mail, till later, and have a good day.

Love you eternally, LOVE KATIE,

OXOXOOXOXOXOXOX
XOXOXOXOXOOXOXO

SUBJECT: Hola mi chiquita Maude!
SENT: 12/9/96 4:32 PM

Hello Maude,

I am taking a nice little break from the dulldrom of reviewing my Spanish to e-mail you. Want to know my day so far? (No, this won't be a brutal Katie letter, by the way.) Well, I woke up to find your letter and Brad's awaiting me. Your letter was the one containing all the pictures. Thank you very much, I'll hang all of them up in my room, especially the nice man one (hee, hee). So, I read those letters, then a short e-mail from Ashley, then set out on my run. It was a big day for me, cause I ran all by myself and I did it (the whole way) no problem whatsoever without my sister for added motivation. For some reason I was all focused today, maybe cause I've decided to study and stuff during this last week before my exam, so I won't fail too miserably, and I won't be as frustrated when I do the day-long tests. The reason I made this decision is because I also got my letter from the school board saying I was signed up for the test, which would consist of math, French, English, and Spanish. The Spanish was a surprise, unexpected I should say, but that's fine. I like Spanish, so I don't mind remembering all the stuff I learnt last year. You know though, when I think about it, I wasn't at all stressed taking the math final last year, cause I felt so confident and I admit somewhat talented, but this is a whole new ballpark. Considering that I don't KNOW the math I'm taking the test on, it's understandable that I'm frustrated. All I'd like to do for math is just show them my final from last year and say, here, that's what I know how to do, can I not take your dumb test now? But that won't happen, so tough, that's life. I think I'm accepting studying better now because I will be in school soon. I don't really feel like it's still summer, so I don't feel all bitter about having to work. Anyway, there's a good way to bore you senseless, talk about school and tests.

Did you guys buy your plane tickets yet? I hope so, I can't wait, in any case. Did you know that you look very pretty in the picture in your room on the cruise? You do, even though I know that right now you're denying it. For some reason, well I understand why actually, but your scuba picture reminds me of La Nuit d'Horreur that you, Ashley and Char made. Remember now?

Isn't it strange how Brad put a note in your letter telling me he was sending me a letter, and his letter came the very same day! Isn't it ironic, as Alanis Morrissette would say (yes, I'm retarded). I'm glad your mom didn't kill you when you got your phone bill for that call, but we have to learn to be shorter I guess, even though it's a lot funner the way we've done it the past two times, long that is. Plus it should be me who calls next time, although I don't know quite when I can do that. My dad still wants us to wait for our first phone bill before we make any big calls (I, of course, haven't made any, but my sister has).

I'm sorry you have so many computer problems. I guess I'm pretty spoiled cause my dad is such a computer man, and he knows how to fix everything, and we have like tons of accounts under our name, which is somehow good. . . . Actually now that I think of it, I really don't care and it's not at all a big deal, but I'll just inform you that my name is spelt Kath-e-rine, not Kathrine. As you can see, it's really quite pointless of me to inform you, but hey, it just came to mind with the envelope to your letter all nearby. I wish Brad was being more mature with Heather and stuff. I really think it would be so great if guys were capable of maturing as fast as girls, cause I'm going to be with guys younger than me this year, and I sure am not expecting a lot of maturity out of them, and that's sad.

You will be proud of me, cause I'm accepting my body more. Careful, I didn't say I accepted my body completely, just more. I realize and can kind of see that I'm losing weight, and although I'm not totally satisfied, I know I shouldn't complain too much. Of course, everyone here is a waif, so it's more difficult to accept, but if anything, that should make you even prouder of me, since I'm learning to accept me here, if not in Canada.

Bye for now, ma chérie!

Grosses Bises, I love you forever!!!

LOVE KATIE

SUBJECT: Dear Ashley
SENT: 14/9/96 11:46 AM

Hello Ash,

Well, I just got your e-mail from Thursday night. Don't ask me how that happened cause it is now Saturday morning over here. We skipped a day or something. Anyway, despite your reassurance about the test, you know I can't de-stress myself. I just have this ultimate dread, and I can't help thinking that I'll fail (which I will), and failing isn't really a problem, cause I want to fail to get into la seconde, but I don't want to fail so much so that they think I should go to la troisième, meaning grade 9. That would be awful, so as dumb as it sounds, I'm just hoping that I don't fail drastically, just barely.

You know what, you should go on that blind date, even if just for the experience of going on a blind date. That way, you can always join in conversations where people talk about their blind dates, whether the story is awful, or wicked, you will at least have a story. But if you're really too lazy, I understand.

Tonight we have to go eat at this friend of my mom's house, who has a 17-year-old son. I don't even care. It's strange cause my parents have all these friends here that have kids our ages, but they're always guys, and I'm sick of it. I WANT TO START SCHOOL, I keep telling myself, only a little bit longer, but I'm still massively impatient. I started writing Brad back last night. He complained about the length of my letters, so I'm going to make this one super long. I might even bring it with me on the first day of school, to escape into writing when I feel incredibly awkward or out of place.

My sister is all happy now because they have "X-files" here, and I had to miss "Party of Five" because of it. I love that show, but it is so sad usually. My sister just told me that Sara becomes some slutty singer and dies of an overdose. Can we depress Katie a little bit more? I'll feel so bad for Billy cause he already lost one love from her doing drugs. He'll be traumatized. And all that for ratings. Yesterday I watched one where he gave Sara a star in the sky, her very own star, and I could honestly have cried cause it was so sweet, and I would love for a guy that I loved, and that loved me, to do that for me. Okay, from this topic, you can see how I really have a life over here, considering I'm revolving around TV. I will say bye now and start a new day. Have a nice day.

LOVE YOU FOREVER,

LOVE KATIE XOXOXOXOXOXOXOXOXO

SUBJECT: Hi again Maude!!!!
SENT: 16/9/96 10:35 AM

Hola Maude,

How are you doing on this fine Monday (assuming you're able to read this on Monday of course)? I just got off the phone with you not more than maybe half an hour ago, and here I am again. I checked the e-mail, and I was so proud cause 5 messages out of the six for today were for me. I got yours of course, one from Toby, one from Ashley, and two from Heather, cool huh? I'm so proud of being a technology woman, it kills me. We had a great conversation today. I hope this morning you weren't too tired, cause I know you had to get up bright and early. You know it will be much better for you when you drive if you can take the car to school, cause then you can sleep in a lot more, you'll love it (how's that for motivation).

Today I don't exactly have an exciting day planned out, just some studying. And I can always spice up my day watching MTV (I love that channel) and listening to all the latest music. Maybe I'll do all kinds of toning exercises, but no running today, I'm feeling much too lazy. So, not too surprisingly, I kind of don't have anything new to say, except I LOVE YOU!!!!!! HOPE YOU HAD A GREAT DAY,

AND REMEMBERED TO FEED OFF MY POSITIVE VIBES!!!!!!!!

Oh yeah, guess what my mom is doing today? She's going to the new big national library in Paris, to interpret a tour of it, to the mayor OF CHICAGO!!! The mayor of Paris and the justice minister of France will be there too. Pretty good for her first conference, don't you think? Well, I'm going to depart, and respond to the other e-mails, so remember what I told you before (the stuff in capital letters, and stuff we talked about on the phone too) and be happy! I'll talk to you soon,

Love Forever and Ever,

Grosses bises, Katie

XOXOXOXOOXOOXOXOXOXOOXOXOXOXOXOX
OXOXOXOXOXOXOXOXOXOXOXOXOXOXOXOX
OXOXOXOXOXOXOXOXOXOXOXOXOXOXOXO, etc.

SUBJECT: Hola mi amiga, who also happens to be my twin
SENT: 16/9/96 10:39 AM

Hi Heather,

Pretty original subject, don't you think? I thought so. Anyway, what's up, homie? I got your two e-mails today. I was ecstatic to hear from you (I'm such an expressive girl don't you think). I'm now going to use my little highlighting technique on you, which I've already used with Maude and Ashley. Hold up. . . .

Okay I think you've waited long enough, I'm starting dancing! (again) Are you proud of me?

YES!!!!!!! I'm SO proud of you! What kind of dancing are you taking? Are you taking it with anyone you know, or are you being all independent, and doing it by yourself?

You'll have to give me details when you get started, about the people you meet, and stuff like that, kay! ANYWAY, good for you, and I hope it makes you happy.

I can't believe Brad is wearing an earring now!!! I'm in shock, I never thought he would do that again to be honest with you. I'm going to have to harass him about that now of course. I hope that this feeling of yours of still wanting him gets settled soon, either by getting him again (which actually might not be that good), or by finding some other wicked guy to fill his shoes, and then some! (if you understand what I mean). Now that you have dancing, at least it will give you something more to concentrate on that'll be good for you. I'm sorry you hate school, I can't

Katie and Heather

blame you, it sounds like a blast all that work, but as I've told you before, console yourself with the fact that I will be getting much more eventually, and we'll be feeling stressed out together.

So, you keep in touch, girlie, as will I. Have a good day!!!!!!!!!! I MISS YOU TONS AND LOVE YOU EVEN MORE!!!!!!! AND THAT'S A PROMISE!!!

LOVE KATIE

XOXOXOXOXOXOXOXOOXOOXOXOXOXO

XOXOOXOXOXOXOXOXOXOXOOXOXOXO

XOXOOXOOXOXOOXOXOXOXOO, etc.

SUBJECT: Hello my dear Ashley
SENT: 16/9/96 12:56 PM

Hello Ashley,

It is Monday, middayish, and I am writing you back as I got your e-mail this morning. I also got the message from you and Heather at her house, when you told me about *White Squall*, I KNOW, it is SO sad!!! I felt so bad for the man who had to leave his wife, and for the wife who was left, and for the extreme hot guy whom I loved, Paul or some P name, that got stuck. It was so sad. Remember I told you I cried in that movie? I think that's pretty exceptional if it moved me to that point. I know what you mean about it adding to your fear too, cause ALTHOUGH I don't think I really have a fear, I would if I was REALLY far out in the water, in an ocean mostly, and if there was ever a storm, I'd die of fear probably. But let's not think about that too much, cause there's no need for me to make it even worse for you.

I talked to Maude this morning (last night for you), and she updated me on a lot of the cool gossip going around about you know who. It is so stupid and it is not something

I would have ever expected from that one a year ago. Things change. By the end of grade twelve, I wonder just how many of our friends will have gone that far, sex-wise if you know what I mean. It doesn't look like this whole "educating" people about the risks is doing much for our generation. That's kind of sad. I mean it's their choice completely, but it surprises me how many people just give in almost. Some cases are different than others, that's true, but still, where are a lot of their brains?

I never told you this, but this topic of sex is upsetting me and I feel like I have to tell someone, except I feel bad cause it's not for me to tell. Don't stress too much, it's no one you know that well. Anyway, I know someone who did that whole thing, and ended up massively regretting it, but I think she did it because she was having severe emotional, self-esteem problems. Well, in July she wrote me a letter, and it is so sad, because I mean she was my childhood best friend, and as kids we always said that we were against all that stuff, and of course, we didn't seriously believe anything bad could happen to us. Well, the same guy that she made the mistake of getting involved with once, raped her. I couldn't believe it, I mean that kind of thing really just happens to people you don't know and stuff, but apparently not. It shook me up, but in the letter she told me she is doing well, and that she has therapy, but at the same time she is helping herself, and she is building her self-esteem and stuff. She seemed okay, but I was still like "WHY?" you know. Why are we all so blind to the consequences things like that can have on our lives? Obviously I don't think it's her fault she was raped or anything, but from what she told me about the guy from the very beginning, it was obvious he was bad news, and that he was a real jerk. After all these stories, I almost don't know if I'll trust myself to make big decisions like that, cause what if I'm blind too? It scares me a bit, but it also makes me mad, cause we shouldn't have to deal with this stuff. I don't know what I'm saying anymore. You know when your thoughts and words get confused, and you don't even understand what you mean anymore? That's me, so I think I'll get my mind off this topic.

Anyway, good for you for joining the French Club, maybe you'll get better than me in French! (Hee, hee, I'm so cruel.) No really, it's a good idea.

I had the worst dream about French school last night, but you know what? I think that's good. That sounds warped, of course, but you see if I expect the worst, inevitably it has to be better than what I expected. I know you're going to tell me to be positive, but this is my way of doing that. I'm positive it's going to be better than what I have imagined for myself. So it better be, or I'll have to fly home right away.

By the way, your e-mail was very sweet. I'll have you know that everything you said, like how we're still the best of best friends and everything, goes double for me. See, this separation isn't hurting our relationship at all, it's forcing it to adjust and adapt to different circumstances, which will help with our futures cause we will for sure be seeing a lot of changes eventually. I must always have a computer in any case. Well, I have to go live my life now, so I will talk to you later, kay! Hope you have or had a great Monday, and that you smiled and were truly happy at some moments (all moments would be better, but hey, you're not God, neither am I for that matter, so we'll start slowly).

LOVE YOU FOREVER MY FRATERNAL SOUL TWIN!!!!!!!!!!!!

Love Moi, Grosses Bises, Katherine
(I have to get used to writing it)
OXOXOXOXOXOXOXOXOXOXOOXXOXOXOX
OXOXOXOXOXOXOXOXOXOXOXOOXOXOXOXO
XOXOXOXOXOXOOXXOXOXOOXOXO, etc.!

SUBJECT: Hey Ash
SENT: 17/9/96 5:26 PM

Hello there my friend (remember when Erin and Jen always said that at our camp?),

Anyway, how was your Tuesday? I went with my sister to see about her getting babysitting jobs here, and she will now most likely have one every day, except Wednesdays, after school for about two hours. She'll be rich, cause here they pay about ten bucks an hour. Of course, as is my nature, I'm jealous cause everything is working so peachy for her, and everything seems to go wrong for me. It's so frustrating. Last night I couldn't sleep. I think I might have slightly experienced an anxiety attack, or something. I honestly couldn't even close my eyes, and my whole body was tense and all strung up, cause I couldn't stop thinking about all the bad stuff that could happen, and about all kinds of stress I'm feeling right now.

You know what? My mom decided that if she makes more money this year than she expected (which is actually possible), during our vacations in February, we might go to Greece. I think that would be really neat for us, but there is absolutely no guarantee. Did I tell you my mom has been interpreting for big important people? Well, she already did a tour of the national library, interpreting for the mayor of Chicago, for the mayor of Paris, and the finance minister. On Thursday (the day of my test, TWO DAYS!!!!) she is doing a press conference, with all the reporters and photographers, for the president of Apple Corp., like the computers. I'm proud of her, but she's really scared. I never realized how difficult interpreting is.

My feet super hurt right now, I've been wearing high heel sandals all day. Anyway I think I'm going to die of stress soon, of course I'm exaggerating, but what can I say,

I WANT THAT TEST OVER WITH!!!!!!! So, be happy, baby, and sorry my message is all retarded today, but my mind is super stressed so it's difficult to focus. I'll be perfect in a few days, I promise, kay? I'll talk to you later,

XOXOXOXOOXOXOXOXOXOOXOXOXOXOXOXOXOXOOXOXOX OXOOXOXOXOXOXOXOXOXOXOXOXOXOXOXOXOXOXOXOOX OXOXOXOXOXO, etc.

Love Forever, Katie

SUBJECT: Hi Maudie!!
SENT: 18/9/96 8:14 PM

Hi girl,

I just wanted to send a little e-mail to say hello, and how are you? Actually I also wanted to do something other than stress about the test tomorrow. It's nighttime, and I spent all day reviewing my math from last year, and reading my French stuff from this summer. Then I made the big mistake of looking at the math they gave me here, and felt completely lost again. So I'm going to fail that, but that's no new news, so I guess I'll have to accept it. So how is nifty little St. Mary's doing? You should see how hard I am trying to get my mind off this test.

Do you wanna know how obsessed my sister is with the show "Highlander"? SO OBSESSED, that's how much. It's really annoying too. EVERY night, we HAVE to watch "Highlander," or she'll DIE! Tell me that's not sad for living in Paris. I just thought I'd tell you that, cause of course it's on right now, and I'm sick of TV.

Let me think, what other stupid facts can I tell you? Oh yeah, I never told anyone cause it's so dumb and pointless, but since I'm looking for things to think about, guess what? Well, at the very beginning of summer, our CD player (the portable one that plays tapes too) died. It sucks cause I can't escape into music in my room anymore, not the way I like to anyway. Times like tonight, where I would just lie there, and not think about anything except the music. Oh well, that's something I'll appreciate when I get home (of course we'll buy a new one now!). Also, my trusty calculator that has seen me through lots of rocky times died the very first time I tried to use it in France. So, I attempted to understand my sister's, but it's just not the same and it doesn't do fractions, which really blows for little ol' dependent me. Now that I think about it, I wish this country would stop killing my electronics (our printer too).

I am so irritable right now. These last three months I've been trying to acknowledge my bad points, instead of denying their existence, and being dumb. You're probably thinking, "NO, NO, NO, you shouldn't do that Katie," but really, it just brings me a step closer to self-improvement cause I have an idea of what needs to be worked on, or changed, you see? Anyway, all that to say, I'm an irritable person a lot of the time, usually when things aren't going my way. I will list my other bad points now, so I will have them written down so I can't forget, or maybe when I get back from France, I'll look at the list and have myself a good laugh, cause I will by then be perfect (just kidding).

So, I can also be very jealous and possessive when I believe someone or something is mine (I know, it's pathetic), and I can be pretty selfish a lot of the times, without realizing it (the whole denial problem), but sometimes I catch myself, and I assure you, I try to improve. I expect too much out of myself, and my life, and worry myself sick sometimes about things I can't change, or that I should just leave alone. Despite my recent advances in optimism and being positive (that's cause I'm working on it), I think I might be a pessimist at heart who needs to break free from that world. You get? I'm also a loser, but that is in the eye of the beholder, so sometimes I don't think I am. That's all I can think of right now. Are you enjoying this e-mail so far? Don't worry, I'm not trying to be morbid, and I'm not unhappy, but I'm stressed, and sick of this, as the French say, "J'en ai marre" of this whole waiting game I've been playing for nearly three months here. You can understand that tomorrow would stress me out, because my whole year rides on this test, and I feel powerless in the world of French administrations. By tomorrow though, when I e-mail you, hopefully I will say, "I did it! And it was fine! And I will soon have a life!" So I'll cross my fingers, and you cross yours, alrighty my dear?

Well, I hate to leave you, but I will e-mail Ashley too while I'm at it, seeing that the apartment is empty, save for my sister having a bath. After I will get lost in some music in the living room, where luckily there is a working CD player (the people who lived here's CD player). So ta-ta ma chère, grosses bises, et fais de beaux rêves cette nuit,

D'une de tes meilleures amies, Katherine

XOXOXOXOXOXOXOXOXOXOXOXOXOXOXOXO
OXOXOXOXOXOXOXOXOXOXOXOXOXO, etc.,

Love Katie (I have multiple
personalities, ha, ha, ha)

SUBJECT: Hi Ashley!
SENT: 18/9/96 8:27 PM

HI ASHLEY,

Well, of course it's me, who else would it be e-mailing you from PARIS, you fool! Just kidding, I'm being a mongo dork tonight because I am desperately trying to get my mind off the fact that I have a big test to write tomorrow, and that my year depends on it. Soon the unknown will no longer exist, and I'll have to see to the even more frightening task of going to my first day of school. But let's not go that far yet, cause tomorrow is not over yet. So dollface, what's new? Having a blast within the heart of St. Mary's High School I suppose (I'm sorry, that was cruel). No, but really, I hope you still smile occasionally when you're there, because I have this horrible image of you last year, sulking against lockers, and if it's the same case this year, I'm not even there to put you in a worse mood by saying you look snobby! (Just kidding, you know I love you, plus my intention was to make you laugh. If I failed, I will try again.)

OOO, oo, oo, guess what? My cousin (Lisa) is moving onto an acreage with her aunt and uncle in the spring (same time that my other cousins that are just moving there will be having their baby), and I have a feeling it's by your house somewhere, maybe. I could be totally wrong, and this might be of no interest to you, but I wanted to tell you anyway. Plus, I was thinking about how when I come back, I might have another cousin. My grandparents have probably started the process of opening files, or whatever, to find that lost cousin of ours that was given up for adoption. That would be so weird if they found her, or vice versa, and we wouldn't be our grandparents' only grandkids anymore. Wow, I wonder if it will ever happen?

Well, I'm sorry to do this to you, but I'm off to escape into music, and to . . . well, I don't think I'll do anything else except worry, but that's life. So adiós mi amiga, te quiero mucho, y mi nombre es Katie (sorry, I had to throw that in to practice some Spanish before the test!) Love you forever (and a day), that's a cute saying, huh?

Love moi, KATIE

Do You Ever Go "Where's Katie?"

★ ★ ★

SUBJECT: Hi Ashley
SENT: 19/9/96 8:35 PM

Hi dearie,

Well, I'm not making this a big e-mail, cause I don't have the heart for it today, and besides which, I wrote you a letter during the test that I will send you (let Maude and Heather read it too if you want) tomorrow. In short, thanks for all your good lucks, but I failed anyway.

I can't say I really had a good day, no one in my family did. You should have seen the uppity atmosphere at home (hint of sarcasm). After dinner we sat around the table for a long time, just talking, to try and raise the morale. I'll just tell you, despite my urge to start a life dès que possible, I won't get the results till Sept. 28, and then we'll have the whole process of "finding me a school" to go to, and frankly, I don't anticipate going any time soon. I understand their game now. So, I was about to lose it, but we had our little family talk, and I'm trying to put it out of my mind.

I think I have decided to go out as much as possible till then, with my sister or whatever, and do as much stuff as possible to fill my days. I'm sick of TV, and of this apartment. Maybe now when guys try to talk to me, I will talk back, just for the sake of having conversations. Who cares if they're perverts, I'll practice bashing them (jk). No really, after all this, tonight I'm going to try to meditate, and tell myself all those positive things I want to live by. It'll be hard, but I have to learn how to be strong.

I did meet some people today, but no one I really connected with. This one girl wanted my number, so I gave it, and she took mine, but for some reason, I don't feel like we'll ever be friends. I don't know if she's my type of person, but we probably won't communicate anyway, and she lives on the other side of the city (and it's a big city I might add). Well, I have to forget this day, so I'll stop writing about it right about now.

How was your day? I was kind of just wondering, can you tell a difference in school without me there? I mean, it would be understandable if you didn't, and you're probably already adapted, but like do you ever go "Where's Katie?" or something like that. Feel free to answer honestly. I just ask cause, I don't know why actually, it just came to mind. Well, I think I will go try to help my mommy right now (she had her thing today and didn't exactly have fun, and she has to interpret the next two days too). Adiós mi amiga, hasta luego, mucho AMOUR (slipped a French word in there, ha, ha). By the way, are you coming to France, or what? Keep me informed. I miss you tons and tons, and love you forever,

LOVE KATIE
XOXOXOXOXOXOXOXOXOXOXOXOXOXOXOXO
XOXOXOXOXOXOXOXOXOXOXOXOXOXOXOXO
XOXOXOXOOXOXOXOXOXOXXOOXXO, etc.

SEPTEMBER 19, 1996

Hi Ashley,

This is so weird, I'm writing you a letter during these retarded tests cause I have absolutely nothing to do. Why, you ask? Cause English was so easy, and I still have like an hour and 15 minutes. So I'll tell you about my day. I woke up, read your e-mail (it was like 6:30), thanks by the way, and had two yummy croissants that my mom got me. Amazingly, I wasn't at all nervous, I just didn't think up a plan of action. When I was all ready, it was like 7:30, both me and my dad got in the car and drove to the high school, where my exams obviously are. Now, I was feeling completely inadequate going past all the young people, although I don't know why. My dad and I found this room, and I was like the only test person here yet, so my dad left, and I waited outside. I was standing there, pretending to be really interested in my nails, then these three girls walked by and looked at the room like "Why are they having tests here?" So, of course they ask me, and I fumble over my awkward sentences and tell them. So actually they were nice, and they asked me where I was from (I said Canada, duh) and wished me good luck. So I felt a bit better.

So I waited until some creep-looking man opened the door and let us go in. There are 27 other people in this room as I'm writing. It turns out this man is our supervisor, and he is following to a "т" the French attitude (maybe it's just Parisian) that I've observed so far. He couldn't care less about us. So, people keep giving me super weird looks cause I'm writing and I'm not doing English. I say, who cares, cause I'm done. I actually can't believe they're taking this long. Could I have missed something? If I did, oh well, I'd rather write to you.

Where was I? Oh yeah, I failed math. Just for kicks I will send you the questions I had to answer. Maybe after grade eleven math it will make sense to you, but for me, it could have been Chinese. Well, not all of it, but let's say I completely missed question (exercise) 2 and 3.

I just made a fool of myself, you should see how red my face is. Some guy just asked if someone had an "effaceur," so I gave him my eraser. Silly me, that's a "gomme" and they all think I'm really brainless. What if, after this year, my face is permanently pigmented red from all my embarrassments, that would suck.

Okay, I'm over it. I don't know these people and will never see them again, right! I am seriously thinking that I missed something in the English. If I did, it would be because I don't understand the French instructions, of course. Then I'd feel sheepish. Why are they taking so long? They make me sick! I'm just a little Canadian lost among all these whatever-they-are's!

Anyway, I failed math, and I didn't do that well in French. Spanish is next, and I'm a dead duck for that one! Actually, if it's like the English, which is easy (I know I have an advantage though), I'll probably still fail. In short, I don't think I'll be going to la première (grade 11), it's la seconde for me (grade 10) looks like! I already knew that though, so it's no big blow. You know what's retarded? They specifically said that we were not allowed to bring calculators, but when we got here, they said okay. HELLO! Guess who left hers at home like the good little girl that she is, MOI, of course. So, I had to mentally calculate, whereas I could hear all these calculator-happy fingers tapping away.

My thumb hurts. After today I will be a thumb cripple. I think I sprained some thumb ligaments. I think it would be really funny if I started laughing hysterically right now, and all these people would think I was insane. Plus the teacher would look at me and get all huffy puffy, and I would just laugh and laugh. Yeah, right, I may have the urge, but little old me would never ridiculise herself in that way.

Oh-Oh, Oh-Oh, no! There's this girl that I've been talking to, and who I had lunch with, that is now going to the nurse's place cause she feels sick. I don't mean to sound materialistic, but she's wearing my jacket! How am I supposed to find her after?

You know, I could have lunched with four different people today: my daddy, the girl Estelle (who I ended up with), or these two guys who seemed like they were going to ask me, till I said my dad was coming. Then I ditched my dad for the girl, but the guys only saw me with her after, so they probably think I'm evil now for lying. Such is life, except that there's one who is <u>really</u> not bad (that was going to ask me), but like I said, I probably won't see any of them again.

So, to the high school atmosphere now. This place is brimming with teenagers, and a lot of them are super hotties. But I wouldn't want to go to school here, cause for some reason this one doesn't appeal to me at all (sure the guys are okay, but who said I'd ever get to know them). Wow! I think I started a trend! Other people who are done their English (finally) are starting to write stuff on scrap paper too. I'm serious (jump in topics), my thumb <u>really</u> hurts. You should see how gibbled my hand looks as I'm writing right now. I need a little break, sorry.

That's enough (two seconds passed by). I think when I'm writing Spanish, I'm going to pretend you're beside me and helping me make up things to write. That'll be fun, huh? Oh yeah, I ate in a typical French-style cafeteria (school one) today. It was weird, they don't have round tables like St. Mary's. The whole room somehow reminded me of all those American shows, with teenagers sitting at tables in the cafeteria. Do you have the picture? Just typicalness, it was packed, and I was worried we'd have to ask people if "spots were taken," but we found a nearly empty table and just sat. I totally like our (Mary's) cafeteria better, it's so friendly and fun (you probably don't agree with me).

I don't even care that I probably failed. I think it's better for me, but IF they try to put me in grade nine, I'm going home. Oh, teacher switch. This one may come around and look at what people have done. He'll probably wonder what I'm writing on these scraps that would take up so much room. Oh-oh (I say that a lot, don't I), I think the girl who has my coat (she's back now) wants me to cheat for her and do her English. I don't understand (pause right there), I did it, I feel so bad now. Oh God, I just gave her one of my papers. Why am I so passive! I don't even say no! Plus now I really have the impression I missed something big in the English thing. I feel like such a dork, a cheater, and just overall evil!

Just let this day be over! I can't believe I misunderstood the instructions! If I fail English, well, that will just take the cake! Please God, I hope I didn't, cause I don't think I will ever know a greater shame than that if it is so. (Well, that's doubtful, cause we're talking about me, and I still have my whole life ahead of me to be embarrassed.)

I am bored! I feel stupid! I failed everything! Life just sucks! That's almost like a little poem, you know, it just flows. I feel so guilty for aiding a cheater. Why am I such a weakling, I ask you? The people around me probably all think so badly of me. Oh-oh, scary man teacher is back. If he sees my paper on her desk, I'm dead. I will pray to my angels now. On top of all this, it's Spanish soon. I Wanna

Go Home (as in Calgary at the moment). I think I might be a very usable person, that's scary. It's actually giving me chills, don't let me get used, kay, if you can prevent it that is. I just drew my little symbols, and people are all curious as to why I was so huddled over my page. I am just such a mystery. It's our break now, I should probably go out and be social, or else they'll keep thinking I'm a snob. Catch ya later!

Hi, I'm home now, and I've already e-mailed you. I failed to tell you about Spanish. Well, I went on my break, went to the ladies room, where they conveniently had no toilet paper (it's all so primitive), and so I held it (that sounds so icky, but I didn't have to go THAT bad). I came back and slightly chitchatted with some people outdoors, then creep-man made us go back. Then came (imagine a drum-roll) Spanish! How was it you ask? Imagine this, he gives me the paper, I look, and automatically say, "Now there's a fail!" Well no, but that's just to illustrate a point. I liter-ally was going to start writing any Spanish I know, like cómo estás, just to fill my page, so the creepy teacher man wouldn't give me evil looks if I had an empty page, but instead I practically just recopied the text in different orders on the page. Original, don't you think? So, it's safe to say, I BLEW that one, baby.

My sister was just in my room with me, and she had an insanity attack. She was neither crying nor laughing cause it was a bit of both. That's how I feel sometimes too over here. Something my dad said tonight might be very true – life in Calgary will seem SO relaxed and easy after a year in Paris. Maybe grade 12 will feel like a year off! Anyway, I hope all is faring well in your world and that you keep smiling and exuding positiveness, even just to make up for the lack of mine at the moment (our fraternal souls need to have some kind of balance, right?). I just might sleep now and put this day behind me as best I can. Like I said in e-mail, I won't know anything till Sept. 28, so I must find stuff to occupy my time.

Adiós, Ciao, Au revoir, Bye

LOVE KATIE BFF & LYLAS

SUBJECT: Hello Ashley!!!
SENT: 20/9/96 11:08 PM

Well hi there my friend,

I have to send you a short e-mail. I would write long today except I'm exhausted. My mom needs to go to bed too for her work tomorrow, and since this computer is in her room, I kind of have to get off. Briefly though, today I took advantage of the whole Paris situation and my sister and I went to the Palais de la Découverte, which is neat and has all these cool experiments (like our planetarium). We also went to their planetarium with a big screen that surrounds you and shows you the stars, although the one in Calgary is better. It's a place where all the discoveries of the world are kind of recorded, or pretty close at least. Some of the stuff wasn't that interesting (it depends on what you're into), but it was something I wanted to be sure to see before the end of this year, so I accomplished something and enjoyed myself.

Tomorrow I'm going to try to be productive too, I don't know how yet, but I'll find something. Look, I'm truly sorry, but I'm dead tired, so I have to leave you (by the way, French channels are now showing shows that would be labeled as pornos in Canada, probably anyway, and I'm just disgusted, cause from here I can see the TV in the living room and I can just see your shocked expression if you were here, watching them, ha, ha, that's a funny thought).

Anyway, I have to go, but I promise to write tomorrow.
Tell me all about your Friday if you want, kay?

> LOVE YOU FOREVER, ON HEAVEN AND EARTH
> (pretty fitting wouldn't you say, my fraternal
> SOUL twin), Adiós, à demain, bonne nuit.
> XOXOXOXOXOXOOXOXOXOXOXOXOXOXO
> XOXOXOXOXOXOXOXOXXOXOXOXOXOXOOX
> OXOXOXOXOXOXOXOXOXOXOXOXOXO, etc.

SUBJECT: Hi my twin!
SENT: 21/9/96 2:22 PM

Hello Heather!

How's it going girlie? I'm writing you this e-mail on
Saturday at 2:20 PM and I'm having quite the blast. I don't
think I will be going out today cause I feel sick. You know
that flu-y feeling, where your head and your muscles all
feel so incredibly tired and dead, that's me. I don't know
what's wrong, but I better be better by tonight cause my
sister and I are going to a movie, whether I collapse or not,
in hopes of meeting people, or just to be surrounded by
them and to get out.

So what are you doing this weekend? Actually I know
you're dancing today cause of your e-mail. Tell me how it
went, kay? I bet you'll feel so graceful after you get into it,
and it will keep you in shape (not that you aren't perfect
as you are), so you won't have to think about not going to
Lindsay Park. Overall, mighty good plan I say.

I assume you know that I wrote my big stressful test
finally, and now I won't know the results till the 28th, so
I'm really going to try to visit all kinds of museums and
stuff before then. I have to take advantage of it, I know. I
just hope I won't be sick. Well, I would love to chat more,
if my head wasn't swimming and my back wasn't so sore,

so it will have to wait till next time. Have a great weekend and I hope to hear from you soon!!!!

LOVE YOU FOREVER AND EVER, MISS YOU TONS!!!!!

LOVE moi!! XOXOXOXOXOXOXOXO, ETC.

SUBJECT: To the girls
SENT: 22/9/96 8:38 PM

Hello Ashley and Maude,

Now in case that doesn't sound like a regular Katie greeting, then you're right! Katie is sick and even though she's practically on her deathbed (okay maybe not that bad – she just feels really crappy), she's so guilt ridden because she hasn't e-mailed you guys ALL weekend, she begged me to write in her place. So that's why her wonderful older sister is writing to you instead of her, although she is going to read this over to be sure that I don't lie too much. She wanted me to bring you up to date on our weekend activities.

Yesterday we didn't do much during the day (I went for an interview for a job that I got!!), and after dinner the whole family went to a movie. Well we took your advice and saw Phenomenon, *and it was phenomenal! (Sorry, I just couldn't help myself!) No really, we loved it – the whole family. I cried from the time that people started turning away from him (George), and didn't stop until the end (I think that it's the same for my mom, but we weren't sitting with them so I can't be sure). My dad didn't cry, but Katie did right at the end. Just in case you were wondering, we saw the movie in English, but it had French subtitles. At any rate, it was a huge success! Then today we all (yes, yet another family activity!) went to the conciergerie, which is Paris' most famous prison (Marie Antoinette was held there before being beheaded). We had a tour guide* who talked at super speed, but we were able to follow (a lot of people couldn't), and he was really very good. The French revolution was a bloody, bloody affair. Don't you guys study that in grade eleven études sociales? Katie says that she almost fainted in there, and I have no problems believing her considering that when I looked at her she was as pale as a ghost (her cheeks weren't even at all red!!), and this has everything to do with the sickness, which is keeping her from writing you herself.

Katie also wanted me to tell you that I met a good-looking guy (at least I think he is – no one else in my family saw him, which leads me to believe that they're all blind!), and next Sunday we're going to meet at the Louvre and explore. What will come of this, who knows? All I care about is that I finally get to go out without any family members!!!!!! I mean I love Katie and my parents, but after 3 months I need a break – Katie feels exactly the same as I do. She also told me to tell you that she'll never meet a guy in that way, but I'm not going to tell you that cause I don't believe it at all – she just loves to have negative thoughts about herself! If you want any more details, ask Katie and she'll tell you when she feels better. In case you're wondering why I'm sending the both of you the same message, the answer is quite simple. I'm simply too tired and overall lazy to say the same thing twice. Well, I hope that everything is going well for you guys and if it's not, please wait until Katie feels better before saying anything cause if there's one thing that I really suck at, it's giving good advice. (I can give bad advice no problem.) Kate's waiting anxiously for your responses. It was nice having a one-sided conversation with both of you and until the next time.

Good-bye! Christelle (a.k.a. Katie's secretary)

SUBJECT: Hey Ashley!!
SENT: 23/9/96 3:11 PM

Hello my dear fraternal soul twin,

How goes it? Just so you know, I'm doing much better now, although my head keeps pounding, and I think I will go see a doctor to see if I have a brain tumor or something (jk). You know me and all my demented health problems, so I guess I don't want to take any chances. Anyway, right now I have Garth Brooks on and it just screams CANADA, it's funny. So how was school today? I can't believe we're already into another week, just like how I can't believe that every week. Last night, I was going to go to bed early, but since I napped earlier, I couldn't, so I read *Embraced by the Light* (the end of it), and then with my sister and my dad, we watched two "ER"s in a row, and parts of *Ghost*, which is such a sad movie, but I didn't want to watch the whole thing, mostly cause of the sadness, and because it was dubbed in French, and it just wasn't right. Like you care, but I'm blabbing so you will have to put up with it.

Your weekend didn't sound bad to me. I know my sister told you about ours. You seriously have no idea how much I loved *Phenomenon*. I am going to buy that movie and the soundtrack when I get back, it is so wicked. I could've cried as much as my sister did, but some psychological thing happens to me when I'm surrounded by people in a sad movie, and I usually hold a heck of a lot back. If I was alone I'm sure I'd be sobbing. Besides that, I've been content this weekend, even when I didn't do much, because why shouldn't I be? Plus for some reason, I'm feeling all in tune with my spirituality lately, and I'm really trying to better myself. A lifetime goal I know, but you have to start somewhere, right?

About your skiing, you were right on the money. You

know darn well what I think you should do, go for it! Like I said, you have to start everything somewhere, and doing this on your own would be a big leap into having initiative, which is going to be super important all throughout your life. The few months I've been here I've totally admired my mom's initiative, and it's something I realize you really have to learn, if you ever want to get what you want out of life. You have to try and take the initiative to call someone, or ask a question, and stuff like that. So, that's a new big Katie goal. I know I have a good role model, so I hope in my future, I will emulate her actions when I'm forced to do things on my own and be independent. If I learnt to do it even before then, it would be good too of course.

About you guys getting your tickets, I'm glad it's getting somewhere! I want you guys to tell me the minute it's confirmed and everything, kay. Although, to be honest with you, I don't mean to offend them, but we would seriously not have room for Andria and Katie. Our car is seriously small (we don't have the van cause it was rented) and you guys (the three of you) are totally the limit we can have in our house at one time. But like you say, they'll probably be too lazy to go through with it, so I'm not too worried about disappointing them, but I just felt I should let you know.

CRAP!!! My pounding headache is coming back full force. I HATE headaches, I never used to get them, so I'm totally bewildered as to why they are plaguing me now. That's life, I guess.

I'm sorry to ask you, and say this to you again, but will you guys talk to my grandma? She called us the other day, and when I said good-bye to her, she seemed to be crying, and my grandpa was all sad too, so I thought maybe it might cheer them up to see my friends they love so much. It's up to you, and I know you feel awkward, so it's a matter of choice, kay. I just felt like bringing it up again.

About your e-mailing problems, from what I can tell, I'm not missing any of yours, and it's only that sometimes I get it twice because you send it to yourself. Don't worry, we'll figure it out. I bet you wished your daddy was a computer man like mine, so you could just ask him, as I always do. Are you excited you'll be getting a letter from me soon? Tell me when you get it kay, but if you're willing, let Maude and Heather read it too, cause I get tons of letters from them too, and I don't want them to think I'm neglecting them, or something. Do you know if Maude has even been able to read or receive my e-mails that I've sent her, even with all her computer problems? I know she has a lot of difficulty sending stuff, but I want to know if she gets the stuff I e-mail her anyway.

You know what, I love God! You're probably gonna start thinking that I'm some super obsessed person with Him and stuff, but I'm not, I just love Him! After reading certain parts of *Embraced* again, the part about how as spirits we choose who to go to earth with, the people who become our family and friends, I was so moved. I truly feel blessed because of my family and you guys, you're so special to me. Sorry for the sappiness, but I get so happy when I think about stuff like that. I miss not being able to have a straightforward conversation with you about this kind of stuff. Even though communicating with words is hard too, I still think I could express myself better. Oh well, we'll have a lot of catching up when we see each other again.

I think I'm going to rip my brains out, if that's what is causing me this pain!!!!!!!! Well, that would be dumb actually, cause then I would no longer be, but I think it would be neat if it was possible to give me a brain massage, and massage out all these poundings, or something. Maybe someone will invent that someday, that would be fun. You should see how big my maternal instincts have been lately (TOTAL switch in topics). I can't wait to be a mother. Despite all the million other things I want to do, I think that will be my favorite. Of course I will be patient, cause my ideal would be to be a mother with a perfect husband (whatever that is) as the father. Well, you never know what life is going to dish out, so I'll just wait and see about all that.

Today was monumental in my life, I completely cut off all my nails so I can start at zero again. Can you believe that I actually had long, even (with each other) nails for nearly two months!!!? I barely can, but now I know I can do it, so I'm proud, plus I could have kept them longer, but I decided I wanted newer healthier nails instead. But of course, now I feel so gibbled and ugly with my hands, but I'll learn to get used to it, I always do, until they're perfect again, that is.

Can you believe my sister's guy story? I am insanely jealous (well, not really, but it adds emotion doesn't it), but I guess eventually my time will come, whether it be in school, or a museum, or something, I'll just have to be patient. Although I think the school atmosphere is much more probable in my case, cause I'm just too wary of strangers, but I guess you never know.

Aren't you glad that I'm not whining about dying from boredom or something? I think that must be a nice change for you, plus I'm not. I'm peaceful and content, despite the raging headache, that is, so I can't complain. Anyway, my dear, I'm departing now, cause I still have my e-mail to Heather to accomplish, and many a Tylenol to take. So adieu, have a great night/day, and be happy, take a little initiative every day, and I'll try to too (how about those driving lessons Ash?). Please answer all my questions, oh wait, one thing I am really missing right now, besides you and the girls, CLEAN AIR!!! I mean you get accustomed to the pollution, but I swear I can't breathe the same over here. I literally can't take in as much air, cause my body probably can't handle all the carbon dioxide or something. Ta-ta in any case, I love you ALWAYS!!!!!!!!!

XOXOXOXOXOX, ETC.

LOVE KATIE

SUBJECT: Hello Heather
SENT: 23/9/96 3:50 PM

Hi Heather,

What's up? How did this wonderful Monday go by for you? Marvelously I hope! (SEE, I still have a retarded vocabulary.) As you probably guessed, not much of your letter was new news to me (although I liked the stuff I already knew all the same) except the possibility that your kitchen might change, and all the details of your braces and dental work. I can't believe the torture you have to go through, but when it's over I know you will be glad, so I'll be glad too.

I'm feeling a bit better right now, except that I still have headaches, which I don't understand (I never used to get them), so I'll probably get it checked out eventually. Nothing new and exciting in my life, although I still plan on taking advantage of this week sometime. Even when I don't go out, I always find tons to do, like cutting off all my nails, which is one of the activities I did today. I'm thinking of it as a new beginning, my nails will grow back as long as before, all nice and healthy, and I'll be all proud again.

I realize that I am a retard. Blame my headachy head for that. I need a doctor for my sick head. Anyway, I've lost my marbles (hee, hee, I'm such a dork).

I hear you guys will be able to get your flight tickets on Oct. 1. Good for you, I can't wait till this whole deal is confirmed. Did you guys decide to go to Montreal with Maude? Talk about French culture shock. It would actually be neat, cause I'm so used to the French accent now, the Quebec accent totally stands out to me. Maybe the same thing will happen to you. Well, I'm going to remedy my sickness with a couple over the counter pills now, so adiós, ma chère amie, and have a blast while you last! (That's a simpleton quote, but it works.) LOVE FOREVER!!!!!!!!

XOXOXOXOXOXOX, etc.,

LOVE Katie

SUBJECT: Hi Ashley
SENT: 24/9/96 6:27 PM

Hi girlie,

So, how was Tuesday for you? As bad as Monday seemed to be? I hope not for your sake.

Guess what? Today my mommy brought me to my doctor here, and I love him, he is so nice I couldn't believe it. I didn't even feel awkward, if you know what I mean. Wait, while I'm thinking about this, have you heard of the Spice Girls, and the song "Wannabe"? Me and my sister have loved that song all summer and stuff, although you know me, I'm getting kind of sick of it, it's on MTV right now, that's what made me think of it. Getting back to the doctor now. So, it so happens that I have colitis. I don't really know what it is, but apparently it's tummy problems related to stress. He gave me all this medication I have to take, even a "tranquilizer" type thing which is supposed to calm me down. I honestly didn't think I was stressed, not to that point anyway. What was really neat though was that he didn't just talk medical stuff. He also asked all kinds of questions about where the stress might come from. My mom told him all about the school situation, and he was all understanding and worried for me, and he said to take this medication till I get the results from my tests, or a bit longer, and maybe by then I'll be less stressed. But he also said if things didn't turn out well, to give him a call, and maybe he could use some connections to help out, although he said there was absolutely no guarantee of that working, but still, that was really nice of him. He scared me a bit though, cause when he was examining me, he hinted first that I might have appendicitis (I don't) and asked if there was diabetes in the family. He obviously didn't conclude that that was the problem though, so I can breathe easy.

Besides that, today my mom, sister, and I went shopping and got new shoes each. You have no idea how out of place I've been here with my Tevas. People automatically think tourist when they see that, and to be honest, I started feeling pretty stupid.

There are SO MANY hot guys in this country. I know a lot of them are slimy, but there really is quite a wide variety of choice down here in comparison to Calgary, not that I really know yet, but that's just something I've decided after looking around, obviously not from personal experience.

Lately, eating's actually really been getting to me cause I have this big hatred relationship with food, which is pretty unlike me, but my reason is that absolutely everything seems to make my tummy hurt, so it really ticks me off, and I get mad at the food. Hopefully the doctor will cure me, and I will be fine and normal again.

Anyway, I have to hang up the clothes to dry now, or my mommy will get annoyed at me, so good-bye, and have a good night.

LOVE FOREVER, Katie
XOXOXOXOXOXOX, etc.

Oh, I forgot to tell you that all the medication the doctor gave me is pills, so I pray to God that I'll be able to swallow them. Maybe this is a big turning point in my life!

SUBJECT: Hi Ashley!
SENT: 25/9/96 6:05 PM

Hi girl,

So how did today go? I'm sorry things aren't all peachy in your corner of the world, but keep in mind that mine are even less peachy. I didn't do anything too exciting today. I went with my sister and her two nanny kids to a movie that was kind of retarded, so a waste of money, but I tell myself at least I went out.

Look, I'm going to address your concerns, then I have a few issues of my own I want to talk about, quite frankly. About you know who, of course you dislike his girlfriend, you see her place as yours, but that doesn't mean you should waste your time with him. You DON'T really like him, and if it bugs you that I'm telling you that, accept it, cause I won't change my opinion. . . . I wish I could "say" all that I'm thinking, cause it would make everything make more sense then. And Ash, you're beautiful, I know you don't believe me or agree, but that is true too, and my opinion won't change there either (neither will anyone else's, who I know all agree with me) so too bad. Just to prove my point, I'd like you to go to some modeling agency sometime and see what they say. My bet is they wouldn't turn you down. Don't stress so much in general, try and see everything in a lighter note (I really am not the one who should be prophesizing this stuff, but I do essentially "believe" in what I'm saying). Try and keep a global perspective for your life, and be aware that life is far from perfect, but we all deal with that, and that what you're dealing with today will be gone tomorrow maybe.

So, I still feel totally sick, my tummy hurts like crazy, my head is always hurting. I feel like a crippled fifty-year-old because of my stupid mattress, and for some reason everything else aches too. I'm not a happy camper. I honestly think that I am creating ulcers as each minute of the day passes. As the French say, Je ne sais plus où j'en suis. I'm so sick of these feelings I've had off and on for three months now, and I want to not worry and to have something legitimate to look forward to when I wake up in the mornings. I don't, I feel like a caged rat in this apartment, and I honestly feel like I'm suffocating. I'm 16!!!!!!!!!! What is WRONG with me??? I feel like I have some terminal illness, that I just can't handle being here, and feeling like I'm never having fun. Truthfully there are very few times in the last three months where I could say that I've had fun. I haven't been depressed or unhappy the whole time, but having fun is another thing altogether from feeling fine, or even happy. All my family ever seems to get is discouraged and stressed with what's going on here, and I feel lost in all this craziness. I might not make sense, but I right now have this big lump in my throat, that I've had about thirteen times today, and I'm so sick of suppressing it, but I have no desire to share it with the rest of my family. Sorry, I'm probably sounding pitiful, but I can't help it, the truth is I feel so alone here.

I know I e-mail you every day, and others too, but it's not the same. I'm so disconnected from life and from all the things that are so important to me. Being with people, talking with people, having fun, they all seem impossible here, nothing's the same. I tell myself it's only a year, and I have to gain all there is to gain in the meantime, but that meantime looks so bleak right now, I can't handle it. There we go, my stomach is churning again, and my head is pounding. It was pretty stupid of me to start thinking about all this.

Actually, I honestly didn't mean to talk about any of that. My issues were going to be something else altogether, but some inner demon took over. Don't take it too seriously, I'm sure I'll bounce back sometime soon. What I was going to say is, well, we have always been blunt friends, I mean we even pride ourselves on that, so I'm just going to say what I have to say. Of course feel free to take into account the fact that I'm really not too chipper right now, and that could totally be throwing me off track.

Anyway, I know you like me to give you input on your life, and its goings on, and I have absolutely no problem with that. I'm always happy that you want my opinion, but the truth is, I kind of want you to do that with me sometimes. I'm not sure how to explain this, so I will try the best I can. When I get an e-mail from you, I feel like everything concerning my life that you comment on is pretty cut and dry, that you say something out of a feeling of obligation to say something about it, but I don't get the impression that you care. Please don't kill me!!! I KNOW you care, and I have many hypotheses as to why you specifically might not want to linger on my life, for my sake maybe even, but the truth is, I'd like it better if you made even stupid comments like, "the doctor sounds nice." Seriously, don't get too offended, cause for me it would have been a lot worse if I said nothing at all, cause I would have the feeling that our friendship was falling apart, and that I was no longer your friend in France who you wanted a "relationship" with, but more like the person you e-mailed to and told your life to, but that was not really living. I have a feeling like I'm digging a hole and getting deeper, but I am purposely not going to erase anything, cause you couldn't do that in a conversation, and that's what I need to feel this is like.

Okay, before I try to explain better, again, I want you to promise me you will truly think about all that I'm saying, or trying to, and get back to me on whether you think I'm being paranoid, or if there is some validity in what I'm saying. Like, do you think that maybe you do, whether subconsciously or what, omit saying stuff about my life cause you don't know what to say, or because you think that you shouldn't have me think about it too much? Look, I think I found the way to describe how this was unsettling me. You know that I give advice to lots of friends, and that I like them, but a lot of the relationships in turn become superficial, cause I do all the listening, and they do all the talking, and they don't really know, or sometimes seem not to care to know, what's up with me. Well, that's what I'm scared is happening. You always say something about my life, like I'm glad you feel better or something, but I feel like you're saying it to get it out of the way. Maybe I expect you to delve deeper and see that I'm not doing better really, and I need you to acknowledge the fact that I am actually living in Paris, trying to have a life, and that it's FAR more difficult than I ever would have imagined. Am I making any sense?

I just reread this stuff, and I wish I thought I was making sufficient sense, but I know I'm not really. I'm truly sorry, but at the bottom of it all, this is bothering me cause when it comes down to it, you and Maude were always essentially the only two I really confided my problems in, and you'd always try to reassure me (even though I know you don't feel really comfortable doing that), and I totally don't feel like that reassurance still exists. There's no one else I feel I can talk to really, so I feel a bit lost. I'm scared that we are distancing, and that by the end of the year our relationship will be like the ones I have with certain people, where it's not nearly as special or genuine as the friendship

I think the two of us have. Like I said though, this might all have been a conscious decision on your part, for my own good, but if it was, I'm informing you that even though I know I shouldn't ponder over my problems, I still need you to ponder over them with me sometimes, do you see? I'm so befuddled it's not even funny. This e-mail will probably be labeled as an absolute horror, like the one I sent Maude, but I don't mean to do that to you guys, I just need you.

Look, I'm going to stop this now, cause I'm losing myself in all these words, and I think you have enough crap to sort through to try and see if you understand what I mean. Again, I'm sorry, but I wouldn't have felt right if I had just let this slide, you know me, little Miss Communication. I don't know what I'd do if I started feeling superficial in our friendship, so try to respond to this, as annoying as it might be. Don't think that this means that I love you any less than before, cause these little things never mean that. I had to get it off my chest, and especially right now, cause my chest always feels like it's on the verge of bursting lately. That was actually quite therapeutic in itself.

Please don't be mad at me for thinking or saying any of this, because you know I didn't mean to offend you, but just to put things out on the table the way I see them. I could be having such a horrible day today that when I wake up tomorrow, I'll think, why was that a problem for me, but this is today, and this is what I needed to deal with. So, I wish I had some funny anecdote to end on a lighter note, but I can't think of anything really, so I LOVE YOU, AND OBVIOUSLY MISS YOU MORE THAN YOU CAN KNOW (I really mean that, sorry I know you wanted me to put off missing you till I got back, but it's really difficult when I have nothing else to do with my time).

LOVE KATIE, From heaven and back

I Love You and Miss You and Hope You're Happy Too

★   ★   ★

SUBJECT: Hi my dear
SENT: 27/9/96 11:06 PM

Hi Ashley!

How are you doing? Are things as dandy as always in your corner of the world? I'm sorry I didn't e-mail the last two days, but to be honest I was scared I ticked you off with my last e-mail, and so I thought I'd wait to see what was going on. Obviously my plans have changed, why you ask, well let me explain.

I woke up early this morning because me, my mom, and my dad were going to go to the rectorat, to see what was up with the whole test issue. So, the story I will tell you will be summed up a lot more quickly than I could tell it, because I REALLY don't want to think about it and get into it that much. Briefly, they told us there that if I didn't pass this test (they still don't have the results), because I'm 16, they won't put me in a school. They're pretty horrible, don't you think? If I didn't make the test then, there's no way any French public school will take me, so we'd have to ask private schools to take me, which costs a lot of

174

money, but like I said, I've had enough thinking about this for now, so that's that. In any case, tomorrow I go see the results of the test, and we'll see where we have to go from there. It's weird cause I never thought it was possible to want to go to school this much.

Anyway, my mom was really not happy when we came back to the apartment. It must have hit me later cause I wasn't at all surprised that something like this would happen, so I was composed, although maybe a little disturbed.

And when I came home, Christelle told me that Maude called, which was good news in itself, and she relayed the message from you, that you weren't mad and stuff, and that you haven't been able to e-mail me because of circumstances, and not out of anger. So that was good, and that's why I'm not scared to e-mail you now.

So now I will move on to other things. GUESS WHAT? You'd be so proud of me if you could see me, I CAN SWALLOW PILLS!!! For the last three days I've swallowed them, all different sizes and shapes, so maybe this time it will stick with me and I'll be able to do it all my life. That will definitely save me a massive amount of sugar calories, don't you think?

This is just offhand info. One of our "family" friends, who is mostly my mom's friend and an interpreter, is tomorrow interpreting for the family of victims of the TWA flight that crashed this summer. That would be quite the sad atmosphere in my opinion.

You should see how incredibly patriotic I'm becoming due to this whole school experience, towards Canada of course, not France. I'm sure France has some good points hidden somewhere, but seriously, it's not what anyone would expect. I realize that even in not thinking about it much before I left, I had a heck of a lot of illusions of what it would be like. Pardon the retardedness of this expression, but, REALITY CHECK. I'm not feeling really bitter or anything right now, I'm just sharing my thoughts with you, because I'm rapidly learning what it means to be a realist, and it's a weird process, where I constantly have thoughts flowing through my head. Actually it feels more like having more insights on life, or something. What sucks is that, with all that I believe, concerning my faith (God), even as it's getting stronger, it's frustrating, cause I don't necessarily feel that it's that much easier to follow my beliefs, to live by them, you know? I mean I do get these moments where I feel like I understand something that I "knew" but couldn't comprehend before all this. And when I feel like I've figured something out, and learned to accept it, somehow, it's just as hard when the same type of issue comes up again, and I have to learn to accept it all over again. I don't know if I sort of forget it or something, or if I just haven't mastered the art, but as I said, it's frustrating to feel like, "Wait, I've been here before, so why isn't it getting easier?" I suppose I have a lack of patience within all this too. I keep telling myself I'm 16, I don't have to have it all figured out yet. It'd be nice all the same, but as usual, I think I'm expecting too much out of the situation.

I think I'm going to start writing this kind of stuff in my journal soon, so I can look back and maybe think, "Good, I think I kind of have more of a hold on that now." So, I'm probably boring you with all this elusive talk, and I'm exhausted, plus I still have to get through tomorrow, so I think I need to rest up a bit.

Oh wait, I just remembered what I wanted to tell you. It's some royal cheese for you, but genuine, so put up with it. During my day, at one of my "end of the rope" moments, for some reason, it came to me all flashlike, if you can understand what I mean, that I was scared of losing you. That doesn't seem like a flashlike thing, but it was the way I felt it. And in that flash, I felt as if we really had been meant to bond together on earth, and I had some earthly fear of losing you. I should have known I wouldn't really be able to explain this in typing words and maybe I wouldn't be able to in real words, but it's true that lately I've been having all this spiritual feeling like flashes, that just make me go "Whoa," or even just smile. I feel all weird saying this to you and not being able to see your expression, like maybe you think I'm going totally insane or something, but at least this way you can get accustomed to it before I get back, with the help of e-mail.

Okay, now I'm really dead, so ciao, I hope you're living life to the best you can, or at least smiling and being happy. I love you always, as you know, and I hope to hear from you (obviously). So, Hurry Up!! (jk, but at the same time not jk)

Hope you have a good night!!!!!!

      LOVE KATIE XOXOXOXOXOXOXOXOXOXO, etc.

SUBJECT: Hello my Beaches correspondent
SENT: 28/9/96 8:55 PM

Hey Ash,

That one was pretty original don't you think, the subject heading I mean. So, how was your Friday? No wait, now it's Saturday for you.

. . . Anyway, about your topic, if the California football guys aren't gone by Monday, like if they're still there, you should talk to them. I don't know why, but you should. You have no idea how much I envy you. You experienced a good school dance and pep rally from what I hear, with hot guys to look at. Oh well, I guess there's just some things I have to miss out on. I'm so proud of you for getting a satellite dish, now you'll be all in on the TV gossip, or at least with the stuff you missed before. But of course, don't let this turn you into a couch potato, cause that would amount to a whole lot of nothing.

By the way, I am soooo hungry but anything except fruits and vegetables disgusts me.

That's something you said in your e-mail, and it's weird, but as my fraternal soul twin, maybe I shouldn't be surprised, but I feel exactly the same way lately. I think my reason though is that absolutely everything I eat, except fruits and vegetables, seems to upset my stomach, which is why I am growing to detest the eating process. I'm sure my situation will change though when my digestion improves (I feel like one of those grandmas that always talks about health problems).

Moving right along, I was surprised, but then again I totally wasn't, that Maude and Matt broke up. I guess cause I always knew when it happened it would be a shock, so it was, but I also always thought it would "go down" like you say it did. We both know Maude has big worries about feeling vulnerable and being subjected to more pain than she feels she can handle, and from the way she always said that they would break up, and that she didn't want to love him, well you catch my drift. Give her a big hug for me anyhow, cause for obvious reasons I can't, and tell her I love her, even if she says she is completely fine. Will you do this for me? I also must admit I feel bad for Matt, but everything needs time to work itself out, and in the end, I'm convinced whatever should happen, will.

About your guy dilemma (hmm, hmm, again?). Just kidding, anyway, you seem to have well-analyzed yourself, but remember what I think is the biggest thing, above all your other points, you tend to want a guy you feel you can't have, and when you have him, lose interest. That's all I have to say, listen closely to your own intuition to see for yourself what direction, or resolution, you should have in this situation, if that made any sense to you. I feel this could be a very long e-mail, if my back doesn't start hurting too much.

Now just to jump around a little, my news for today. With uttermost surprise, I learned today that . . . I failed the test. No big devastating news, since I was aware of that from the very beginning, but now this means all the more stress and frustration for me and my parents, trying to find some private school that will accept me. It's pretty brutal, but you do what you gotta do. My mom has a conference soon on greenhouse gases, and she was asking us all this chemistry stuff, like naming molecular compounds, and believe it or not, I miss it! I miss chem, I rocked so hard core at it, and now I forget mostly everything, and in the meantime you're probably hating it. IT'S WEIRD what life does to you sometimes. In any case, we can't start any hunting till Monday, so my mom is calling everyone she knows for info, help, etc. I spent my day completely not thinking about it.

My sister and I went to the Cité des Sciences et de l'Industrie, which is actually a very interesting, high tech, amusing expos (educational too, of course). So we spent like all day there, we went to the planetarium, to their IMAX theater (which showed an Imax on the sea. That's one that would increase your fear of water, in my opinion anyway), and to lots of interesting expos, that I'm too lazy to get into. The thing is, there were tons of people (it's a big place), but we were totally left alone for once, by guys I mean, at the beginning at least. At one of the expos on the stars and galaxies and stuff, we had the great luck of encountering a posse of homie g's. At first we ignore them, then one of them pretends to be all interested in what we were looking at. So, we casually move away, then they follow us, and they start talking, only two of them. The others were kind of just around. They start asking where we're from, etc., and talking boring crap, so Christelle takes the initiative, and says "Bon, on va continuer à voir maintenant, au revoir." So we walk off in relief, but that feeling doesn't last long. We think we've lost them, but then we enter this dark uninhabited tunnel thing that shows all these planet facts and stuff. Guess who comes in through the other side of the tunnel, the G's of course. So we pretend we don't notice them, and then someone comes up behind me and grabs me (not like a hug, just like my arms, as if he was trying to scare me). Me being incompetent, I just look at him and give him kind of a cold smile. They strike up what they must think is their brilliant conversation again, and Christelle and I are even more distant than the other time (the guys here are really dumb), then I tell Christelle in English that we should go. When we stop talking and pretend to be all interested in the tunnel stuff, the guy who grabbed me keeps following me and looking over my shoulder, as if he cares about what's there. So we get out of the tunnel and the guys come out too. What else could we expect? And then they ask us if we'd like to see them again outside of the Cité des Sciences, as in just "on the town" in Paris. Christelle and I get all awkward cause we hate that question. Then I take the initiative, and just say NO, but nicely (they manipulate very well, cause they know if they're rude and say their true intentions about stuff, we'll be rude right back, but when they act all polite, as if that was their nature, it's hard to be all blunt). They persisted a little, but I was pretty proud and I stood my ground, and we escaped again.

We kept bumping into them after that though, so it was awkward, and Christelle and I were being all wary of where we were going, to make sure that they weren't there. If that wasn't enough, we go down to another level, and there's another guy clan, and one guy steps out and is all like, "I look good in this shirt, don't I?" or something stupid like that, and we just ignore them as best we can, but even when we've descended to another level, they're still saying stuff after us, about coffee or something. Anyway, the situations were a little unnerving, since we're still nincompoops in handling them, and every single time something like that happens I wish I was Erin, who wouldn't feel embarrassed, or shy, and would just say what she wanted to. But we are getting better, so I shouldn't complain too much. Although, in retrospect, the coffee guys seemed like maybe they'd be okay, but it was after the homies (these guys weren't homie gangstas, thank God) so we were very untrusting. Oh well, at least I know they wanted us. I can't wait till I have a controlled environment, meaning school, to meet guys, cause if they're nice, and as good-looking as some I've seen, this year could easily start looking up.

So, can you believe I'm still not in school and it will bientôt be October?! And it probably won't be till later in October too that I do start, and then pretty soon there will be the first two week break over here. I hope I manage to learn enough to graduate grade 12 when I get back, or I will literally shrivel up and die (maybe not quite, but it gets my point across).

I love my grandparents. I just thought about how my mom told them all about our little problem, well, my problem of not having a school to go to, and without my mom even saying anything, they offered to pay for my private school tuition. I don't know if we'll accept, but it would make me feel less guilty, where my parents' stress level is concerned. Plus they are so cute, and my grandpa writes stuff like, how of course they want to help out, after all we're family, and how he thinks we're the best family ever. He's just so cute, and he writes other cute things, and my grandma put my name in her prayer group so I'm just thinking I'm super lucky.

Oh, my sister is just talking about what's on TV to my parents, so it makes me say, they HAVE SUCH A DUMB IMAGE OF CANADA OVER HERE. There's this Air Canada commercial, that makes Canada seem all primitive, as if cowboys and Indians walk the streets, like in the "old" days, and that we all have permanent dog sleds to get around in or something. Well, it's not that bad, it balances itself out at some points, but it is still very exaggerated, and I want to slap them.

Oh well, I guess that's the breaks. I'm sorry, I thought this would be super long, but my back really does hurt a lot, so I think I'll have to depart. I'll just check your e-mail one more time. About Greg calling you Ashtray, which Greg is that? If it's Z., I can just imagine how funny math must be for you, and I think it's fun for you to have a nickname.

I don't know who to be because I feel like I should do this for God because I feel like I owe it to Him except I don't really want to, and as a result I am being incredibly selfish. Look how I create problems for myself.

Yes you do. Don't worry about feeling selfish, you have a right to have experiences, even smoking up, but at the same time you have to know that it would be really bad if you lost your head in all that. Personally, I think you're intelligent, and you wouldn't do more than basically harmless fun every once in a while, so don't give yourself a guilt trip over it, you don't need that. I agree with you anyway, I know the bad sides, and at times I feel like it's all evil of me to do that to myself, but don't ever feel like you're insulting God. You were meant to make your own decisions, and the one you'd rather take of just having fun (but careful) seems totally normal to me. Anyway, that's all I have to say for tonight, today in your case. So bye-bye, have fun, kiss a California hottie for me (if YOU want to, of course, but I have little doubt about that), and write back when you can. Adiós mi amiga.

MUCH LOVE, ALWAYS OF COURSE, Katie

SUBJECT: Hi Heather
SENT: 30/9/96 1:25 PM

Hello my dear,

Well, don't worry, I got both your recent e-mails that told about the wicked pep rally and California football guys. YOU ARE SO LUCKY!!!! I wish I hadn't missed that, but I guess that's life, right? I'll make up for all the fun I'm missing eventually. I still haven't started school, but today we have an appointment with a really close Catholic high school (therefore private and paying) so it's possible that I may start tomorrow if all goes well, but I'm on my guard for hoping too much, so I just say "Who knows." It might be soon in any case. It would be weird, if after all this crap, I ended up going to a Catholic school again. Maybe then St. Mary's wouldn't make me do Religion 25 if I told them I already took it, AND it would be in French. But like I said, there's no guarantees, so I will keep you informed. I heard the big news about Maude and Matt, it's shocking, but then not really. Anyway, I know you and Ashley will be there for her if it starts to get to her, although from what I've been told, she's fine, so that's good.

Oh, I guess I haven't outright answered one of your questions. I did get my test results, and as predicted, I failed, which is why I now have to go to the private system, cause they won't put me anywhere in the public. That's life, I just have to deal with it. As for my being stressed, well, I have been, but when I wrote Brad's letter, I didn't really realize it (if you can believe it), and I only really realized it when I decided to go to a doctor, for health problems, which he told me are all massively stress related. I can't wait for ALL of this to work out so I won't be stressed anymore, that's for sure. Meanwhile, as I STILL sit on my butt, you sound swamped with homework. I pity you, but at the same time I envy you, pretty strange huh?

So, pretty soon you guys will be able to buy your plane tickets, right? I can't wait, tell me the second (almost) that you get them, so I can finally know that you guys are coming for sure. Oh, yeah, I just remembered, did you know that on your b-day, there's a solar eclipse? Pretty cool, huh? I think I will watch it with those little special glasses and think of you. I have a solar eclipse on my birthday in like the year 2007 or something. It's a special event, so if it's possible in your corner of the world, try not to miss it! I'm leaving now, I have tons of crap to do (but I emphasize that it's all CRAP) and I'll just leave you with the thought that I miss you and love you of course.

BYE my twin, Love Katie

SUBJECT: Hi Ashley
SENT: 30/9/96 1:56 PM

Hello my dear,
I am such a fast typer, I can't believe it, I'm pretty proud

of myself I must say. ANYWAY . . . so how did Monday go? Was it just so much fun to be among the St. Mary's villagers, at the beginning of a brand new week? Well, I obviously got your e-mail and thought you should know that you're getting better my dear, if you know what I mean. I keep hearing about all this homework you guys have (Heather told me about hers too), and it's just so weird, cause I have no obligations, no responsibility, and I'm not used to it. Oh well, hopefully (as weird as that sounds) it won't last much longer. Today at 3:00, we have an appointment to meet with the school principal of a Catholic school that's totally nearby, and is of course private. If all goes well, my optimistic parents are thinking I could start school tomorrow, but I'm not gonna give myself false hope, so we'll just have to see. Besides that, I have another doctor's appointment later, and then this girl we barely know from Calgary is coming to stay here. That will be hard cause I'm not in the mood to entertain at all.

Yesterday (Sunday) was a fairly good day, and I just feel like telling you because that way I won't ever forget it. We went to eat at these friends of my parents, whom they haven't seen in like 20 years, and they have four kids. A girl 11, a girl 16, a guy 17, and another girl, 19. It was weird, cause we'd never met them before, but Christelle and I totally talked to the 19-year-old, cause she sat close to us, and she came to this park after lunch with everyone, but the 16- and 17-year-olds couldn't. Anyway, it was strange to be around another 16-year-old girl, cause it's seriously been so long, and she was someone who I could see myself being friends with. In fact, if they lived closer (they live outside of Paris), and we saw more of each other and got comfortable, she totally seems like my type, and the guy seems really nice too. She didn't talk much, but I was totally analyzing her, and I'm way too lazy to explain what I deduced, but I only wish she lived closer. When we were close to leaving, she talked more and told us all this cool stuff, and I saw her room. Don't you think I sound desperate for friends? It was totally not a monumental day, but it was just nice, and I know you totally don't understand what I mean, but oh well.

I don't have much new news, as usual, but I hope you guys are getting all prepared to come to France soon, like say, that you guys are planning on buying your tickets right after Oct. 1. Are your driving plans coming along? I realize you probably don't have much time, with homework, social life and all, but I just wondered. Oh yeah, I personally think it's good that Maude is going to have a

Katie and Christelle walking in
Bagatelle Park six days before Katie dies

chance to experience more guys. I believe what will happen will, but I obviously don't know what is "meant" to happen, so I just think if this is a permanent breakup, she's kind of right to not want to get too attached to anyone else, but if they go out again, I think she needs time to be her own person and to try more guys or something. Somehow it just seems healthy, rather than starting to feel so committed at 16. Well, I have things to do now, people to see (ha, ha), so I will leave now. Have a nice sleep, and evening. LOVE YOU FOREVER AND A MONTH

LOVE KATIE

SUBJECT: Hello Maude!!!!
SENT: 1/10/96 3:33 PM

I'm so glad you're among us e-mailers again!!! Truly, I totally have missed you too lately, a lot, and I was going to e-mail you despite the fact that your e-mail was screwed, in hopes that when it was better, you'd get them anyway. But Ashley told me that you probably wouldn't get them at all, so I didn't. Oh, I'm SOO glad I can communicate with you again, you can't believe how dependent I am on this whole e-mail process now. Don't worry, I never thought you were lying and that your computer was actually okay, and that you just didn't want to e-mail me. I have more faith in you than that!

Okay, now I feel like I have so much to say, but right now I must go to the doctor, so I will save this, and keep writing in a bit (not that you'll notice that I was gone).

Okay, I'm back. I will inform you of my health problems now, although you probably don't care. For like two weeks I've felt awful, fever, headaches, nausea, shooting pains here and there, digestion problems (meaning, tummy aches). Last time I saw this doctor, he told me I had colitis (?) due to stress, and he made me take this medicine. But, that was just for digestion, and while that was getting better, nothing else was getting better. Anyway, that explains today's visit, plus I was getting super paranoid about other stuff. It's weird cause remember last year when I kept being sick during my play, and I had that "delicate" problem, that totally upset me, but ended up being due to a low white blood cell count. Well, I observed the same problem, or what looks like it, in my mouth, so I freaked and got all paranoid, but he says it's bruises or something, nothing serious. Anyway, before I bore you any more, he's determined that I have strep throat, sinusitis, and a "cyst" or something in my knee that if it ever got too big, I'd have to have surgically removed, but I don't really care. And all this, I believe, is due to the fact that I've let myself feel super stressed lately, and I wouldn't be surprised if my white blood cell count was down again, cause my immune system is not working at all. Oh, well, I'll get better in due time.

Oh yeah, Ashley might have told you this, but maybe not, cause it's not exactly exciting, but because of all this, I've moved past the psychological barrier that held me back, and I can now swallow pills! Amazing isn't it, I still feel amazed every time I do it.

Okay, that was a really bad topic, and I'm sorry, but I think when I'm older I'll be one of those people obsessed with their health problems, and talk about them all the time. Just stop me when it gets too much. So, let's move on to your life, which is bound to have more twists and turns in it than my life. So, I'll tell this to you personally, but I wasn't THAT surprised when I found out you broke up with Matt. I believe I totally know where you're coming from, if I'm not completely wrong, and despite the fact that it was your decision, I know it must be so hard. Is there tension between the two of you now? Do his buddies try to talk to you for him? Actually, he probably tries himself from what I can imagine. I feel (I keep saying feel, because that's the best way to express it, and I don't want you to think that I'm being all pretentious like if I just said, "I KNOW" how you feel, get it?) like I know what you're going through now, probably a lot of mixed feelings, but as always I could be wrong. In any case, I told Ashley to give you a hug from me, even if you feel fine, because I want you to know that I think about you, and wish I was there to help you. This is the first time you've ever broken up with anyone, and we both know it was pretty serious for a first relationship, which might screw you up even more. All I can say is, feel free to pour your heart out to me if you need it, and even though that will help in itself, I'll also write back and attempt to give advice, as is my natural inclination anyway (See Maude, I'm not losing my English, how many people do you know that use the word inclination?).

I'm glad that you're keeping yourself busy too, that's important, and always something I think you need. When I get back you'll have to connect me with all your "work" people, or maybe I can just do volunteering, although I have a feeling by grade twelve I'll be dying for money, and I won't know where to go. But, I'm not going to start thinking about that yet, cause this year will bring enough worries.

I think I will come out with my good news, cause then you can feel all special about being the first to know about it. Well, I START SCHOOL TOMORROW!! That's even more amazing than the fact that I can swallow pills, don't you think? I will explain the whole story now. Okay, so yesterday, my mom and I decided to go to a Catholic school that is like right beside us (not even a five minute walk). We had an appointment, so when we were waiting, we were all scared that they would reject me like the entire public system did (I assume you know about that). But when the principal came to bring us into her office, she was totally a nice woman, especially compared to all the people we'd come in contact with up till then. Actually we expected her to say no right away at first, like everyone else, and we hoped we'd win her over eventually. But right away she started saying how she thought this was a good experience for me, and that they had room for me, and I could start as soon as I wanted to. Basically she catered to our every need and answered all our questions, and she even asked if this was to be a year off for me, which implies that if I had said yes, she would have said, okay, and let me do nothing (or almost) all year. Obviously I couldn't say that, so we said how we just have to make me pass, and that there's certain things that I need for equivalencies in Canada. So, she said okay, and said that there would be a lot of options I wouldn't have to deal with, since I don't need them cause I'm not going further in the French system. It's still going to be super hard I think (I'm taking Spanish), but I know that if I was in the public system, they couldn't have cared less about me or my "special" needs, whereas these people are ready to coordinate for me. Tomorrow I only go for two hours, and do nothing basically, from what I understood anyway.

You see, today we made another appointment, but with the school counselor, and I went alone and he showed me around the school, and answered all these questions for me, even though I still don't understand a lot about how this whole system works, but I know these people all seem willing to help me, so I'm not nearly as worried as I would have been in public schools. So, of course, as everyone thought, everything is hopefully turning out the way it was meant to be. Think it's fate that God wanted me to go to a Catholic school? Who knows? Now I only hope the teenagers are nice, and accepting, and fun, and then I'll be a happy camper. I wonder if this changes my vacation dates? I doubt it, but don't let that stop you from buying your tickets soon, cause if my vacation does change, either I'll have more time with you guys, or it might not change anything at all since when you guys are planning on coming, I would be in school anyway. So get to it, and get your tickets!!

I really want to see the Cranberries on November 12 when they come to Paris, that would be so fun, especially if I had friends. You know what else is really good? This school never has classes on Saturday, where it was totally possible with public schools.

By the way, thank you for your cute picture, I'll cherish it of course. And I also think that it's so sweet of you to put my picture in your binders. I'm touched, Maude. I keep wondering if when I see you guys again, when you come here, if I'll cry. I know I didn't when I left, but maybe I'll just be so happy to see you guys again that I'll break down, you never know, right?

The only thing about the whole school thing is that it's seriously so different from Canada, I don't know how incredibly lost I'll be. I can't even explain it to you, cause I know you totally won't understand, through no fault of your own of course. If I get cozy-cozy enough in the school eventually, maybe I'll take my video camera there and just be really cool. All good things come to those who wait, right? I really want to write to Mme Lemire sometime soon, and tell her about this, cause I still want her to like me when I get back, but maybe I'll wait a bit longer. Can you ask her if she got my postcard and tell me (I can't remember if I already asked you that). Well, my head is really hurting, and my bladder wants to burst, so I'll leave

you now. Write back as soon as you can, and remember I
LOVE YOU AND MISS YOU INCREDIBLY!!!!!!!!!!!!!!!

LOVE FOR ALL TIME, KATIE
XOXOXOXOXOXOXOXOXO, ETC.

SUBJECT: Hello my dear Ashley
SENT: 2/10/96 2:17 PM

Well dear,

I especially liked your latest e-mail with all the FLIGHT
DATES!!! Honestly, I'm so happy that things are falling
into place. And I realize that before we know it, it'll be
time! Anyway, about the whole school stuff. Well, if
Maude got her e-mail that I sent her yesterday, I assume
that eventually you will be informed on specifics, but I'll
tell you anyway, my pleasure. So, I'm in. Yup, the principal (who was a totally nice woman) didn't even say no
once. And now that this has happened, everyone, including my doctor, keeps saying how it's such a great school,
and they think this is much better for me. That's fate for
ya. Yesterday, I went for a tour of the school with the
counselor, and it's extremely different, but I think I will
attempt to explain that when I'm used to it and understand everything that's going on.

Now, there is something that is a bit bad about all this.
Don't get me wrong, the school is great, and I'm pretty
sure everything will work out, but the problem is that I
was supposed to start today. And normally I would have,
but under my health circumstances, I couldn't. I was honestly all ready last night, but as you've already been
informed, I've been sick lately, with fever and crap, and
this morning I felt like I was going to faint. And as I was
afraid I would vomit, I decided I didn't want my first day
to be remembered by me as worrying about what if I

fainted or had to run out of the room. So, my mom talked to the counselor man this morning, and nice man that he is, he said not to worry, to come when I'm ready, blah, blah, blah. So, it's almost like I can't get out of this scary cycle of sitting on my butt at the apartment, cause I'm at it again! I'm not that concerned actually, I just would like to stop feeling sick and to move on with this year, but at least now I know it will happen.

This is gross, but it's so incredibly weird that I just have to tell you. On top of certain health issues, I got my rag yesterday, and it is worse than it has ever been in my whole life history. My cramps are brutal, but the worst thing for me is the fact that it's so heavy. I was literally amazed yesterday, cause after two hours with a tampon and a pad (I'm sorry this is so gross), I soaked through mes culottes, my pants, and a chair! Never has this ever happened to me. So, I freaked, my mom called my perfect doctor, and he told me it was stress related when it's unusually heavy. I wish people would stop telling me I'm so stressed, cause then I think it makes me stressed.

Besides all that frustration though, you asked how my life is, and I must say it's looking up. When I feel healthy again, I'll be so happy, AND I'll start school and tell you what it's like of course. Right now, I feel the need to lie down, so, I LOVE YOU AND MISS YOU AND HOPE YOU'RE HAPPY TOO.

LOVE KATIE XOXOXOXOXOXOXOXOX ETC.

SUBJECT: Hello from Katie (kind of)
SENT: 3/10/96 2:53 PM

Katie feels bad cause she can't write you, but she's super sick now. She either has sinus infection+strep throat+cyst on her knee+major bleeding (that time of the month) and major cramps, or else all of this is explained because she has appendicitis. Either way she doesn't feel up to writing, or even to get out of bed, so I'm doing it for her (it's Christelle, by the way). Her school is a Catholic school, but she won't be taught by nuns or have to wear a uniform. Basically it's just like our school – and same as public, except for the religion classes. Everyone there has been really nice, and they understand that Kate's sick and they say to take her time. She'll write you as soon as she can (she just wanted you to have an update and know why she wasn't writing you). I hope school is going good for you – I have a feeling I'm going to have a hard time adjusting to the school life next Monday, but we'll see. Well until next time, Christelle (a.k.a Katie's secretary)

P.S. – I'm sending this message to Heather, Ashley and Maude (yes, we know her computer's screwed, but we thought we might as well give it a try!) because once again I'm lazy, and I have to leave soon to babysit so we're on a limited time budget.

SUBJECT: It's me again
SENT: 4/10/96 3:00 PM

Hello Ashley and Heather,
Just writing super fast to let you know that Kate's been hospitalized. She got so that she couldn't even lift her head off the bed, and she was throwing everything up so she couldn't take her antibiotics to keep the fever down. We brought her there this morning and from the test they've run she has an "angine," which is what hurts her throat and got her defenses down and let the fever take hold. She's also bleeding a lot (monthlies), but the loss of so much blood weakened her as well. They also found that she has a very huge amount of white blood cells that

shouldn't be there. She'll be in the hospital for at least 2 days while they run tests on her to find out what's causing the augmentation of white blood cells. Since she's been admitted she's feeling a little better but very tired and very weak. Well I have to go – please pray for her. I'll keep you both informed (Maude's computer sent our message back, so I'm assuming that she didn't get it). Katie sends you all her love,

Christelle

Susan put down the e-mail message she'd been reading – Christelle's to Katie's friends back home. Memories bombarded her mind in quick succession, coming out of the past, flashing into her head and fading. She was back in that hospital waiting room, saw herself with Christelle, with Joël. She again felt the panic, the disbelief, the frustration of making phone connections – the stunned voices of family, of friends, disjointed phrases connecting their helplessness; memories of the doctor sitting with them; Susan asking, because she had to, "Is Katie going to die?" and the doctor saying, "Yes, she's going to die." Then, finally, the moment of acceptance when they were able to go back to Katie to pour their love into those last moments of her life. If you can accept the inevitable, Susan came to understand, then you can make the most of what's there.

Katie had received last rites by the time the Ourious phoned her friends, who gathered at Maude's house to share their grief. Although it was Saturday morning in Paris, it was Friday evening in Calgary. They talked to each of the girls in turn, all of them overcome, Ashley insisting there was going to be a miracle, Susan saying, "No, there isn't going to be a miracle." At some point,

Susan wasn't sure just when, the girls phoned the hospital and asked to have a phone put in Katie's room so that she could hear their voices. This had not been possible.

Later, after she had got home from Maude's house, Ashley sent an e-mail message to Susan, Joël, and Christelle. In it she said: "When I rode home tonight in the car, Katie was with me. I turned on the radio about halfway home and the first song that came on was 'All By Myself,' the one that Celine Dion sings. Anyway, it was like all those times when my mom would pick up Katie and me after we'd been somewhere and drive her to your alley and she would sit in the backseat. I felt like she was there and I opened my mind and my heart to her so I could hear what she wanted to say. She told me that she was happy and that she was like an angel. Then the song 'One more Night' came on the radio, the one I always played on the piano. She kind of came into my mind then and I saw her standing in all this light. I have been a little scared because I have never pictured my future without her in it, but I felt her saying, it's okay, everything is all right. And she is fine. She feels whole and completely complete. I know I have to be strong and we all do because she is happy. I think she wants us more than anything to be strong." They had been comforted by Ashley's experience, more than they had thought possible. To be strong. That's what they were working on.

Susan turned once again to the correspondence, Christelle's final e-mail to the girls. She had written to confirm when they were bringing Katie home for the funeral, and to say that they couldn't wait to see the girls and to hug them. Near the end of her message Christelle had written: **"It means a lot to me that Katie had friends as good as you. Her life was short, but she'd found what** *a lot of people spend their whole life looking for – true friends who love her unconditionally."*

Stated so matter-of-factly, Susan could see that it was absolutely true. Her attention drifted from the stack of papers to the window. She watched autumn rain pelt the glass, heard the wind rush. She felt the muscles in her face soften, relax. It might be possible to smile again, she thought.

Sharing Katie

* * *

FROM AN E-MAIL MESSAGE TO THE OURIOUS FROM MAUDE, NOVEMBER, 1996:

Hi everyone,

I don't really have much to write about, but I'm feeling really down right now and Ashley is at a driving lesson and Heather, well, no one at her house is answering the phone. I'm just sitting here and for some reason I have this feeling of complete emptiness. Don't fret, because I know my life is good and I know Katie is with me and I know that I need to go on with my life and all that stuff I've heard over a million times. Anyway, I feel like I'm in this state of shock, it's like her death has hit me again. It's sometimes hard to realize that even though she is with me, I can't touch her and she can't touch me. I can't just pick up the phone and talk to her anymore!!! It's weird because it seems like just yesterday that she passed away, but it also seems like just yesterday that I talked to her or that I e-mailed her. Yet, at the same time, it feels like this pain has almost been an eternity. I know it is slowly going away, but it's so "to the point" or pungent. I don't know if I'm making much sense to you. It's like I have this massive tight tumor deep in my heart that I wish so much someone would just tear out of me. I feel that my head can't even think straight sometimes because there is always so much going on and it's so energy-consuming to concentrate on things. I hate how this feeling always finds a way of creeping up on me. And I hate to be so evil, but I'm so sick of people telling me to find her in my heart and to pray to her and to go on with life. I know all this!!! I feel her presence and her strength so much in me. I know she is happy and peaceful with God, but can't they just let me cry?

It's almost like every time I'm down everybody presumes I have this whole negative train of thought running through me, but honestly, it's not that. I just miss her. I'm not questioning anymore, and I'm not angry, I just miss her and it's as simple as that. Anyway, I'm going to take a bath now. Please don't worry because I will be fine. It's just one of those days, and I chose you to tell. Thank you, take care, and I love you.

Miss you, and Katie as well.

Love Always,

Maude

XOXOXO

FROM AN E-MAIL MESSAGE FROM ASHLEY, APRIL 1997:

Dear Susan and Joël,

I just got your message today, and I don't know if Maude and Heather got theirs, but I'll be sure to pass on the good news about the book. Well, I want to start off by saying I'm so excited about this whole book thing. If it actually happens, I would love to help in any way that I can, although if that is not necessary, I am just as eager beaver to watch the whole process. I am absolutely positive Katie would be and is eccstatic about it (sorry if eccstatic is spelled incorrectly, but I know you are well aware of my slite handicap, and if it is right, well, we have lost nothing except precious moments reading this babble). Anyway, when I think of this book, my personal reason for being especially happy is that I have trouble remembering things. This book could be really great for everyone and I think it could help me deal with some things.

I also wanted to say that I don't think you should let this be a reminder that Katie is not here. This book could be used to explain where she is right now. I think that, essentially, Katie is where she always wanted to be, although she got there a little sooner than she expected. I think that the large amount of growing Katie did, spiritually, emotionally, and mentally is recorded in those pages and took place during a time when the lucky few of us were very familiar with who she was. I think this book could share that.

You may have noticed a little change of heart in me. I've kind of been coming to terms with the idea of letting her go. Right after Katie's death I realized that we are on our own. Before, I think I confused the idea of loving with never being alone.

I hope this doesn't come across as scattered, as it sometimes does. I appreciate you asking for my thoughts and letting me know what is going on. It kind of tells me that you know how much I love her and that everything is really important to me.

Love Ashley

The End

Katie and Christelle as angels

SOUTH CENTRAL REGIONAL LIBRARY

3⁰⁰
9,49/
4,49
Fri